A Mile
in My Shoes

A Mile in My Shoes

Cultivating Compassion

TREVOR HUDSON

UPPER
ROOM BOOKS®
NASHVILLE

A MILE IN MY SHOES: CULTIVATING COMPASSION
© 2005 by Trevor Hudson
All rights reserved.

Originally published as *Compassionate Caring: A Daily Pilgrimage of Pain and Hope*, by Eagle, an imprint of Inter Publishing Service (IPS) Ltd, PO Box 530, Guildford, Surrey GU2 5FH.

Cover design: Gore Studio / www.GoreStudio.com
Cover photo: © Peter Dazeley / Image Bank
Second printing: 2006

LIBRARY OF CONGRESS CATALOGING-IN-PUBLICATION DATA
Hudson, Trevor, 1951–
    [Compassionate caring]
    A mile in my shoes: cultivating compassion / Trevor Hudson.
        p. cm.
    Originally published: Compassionate caring: a daily pilgrimage of pain and hope. Guildford, Surrey: Eagle, 1999.
    Includes bibliographical references.
    13-digit   ISBN 978-0-8358-9815-7
    10-digit   ISBN 0-8358-9815-6
    1. Pilgrims and pilgrimages. 2. Compassion—Religious aspects—Christianity. 3. Suffering—Religious aspects—Christianity. I. Title
BV5067.H83 2005
241'.4—dc22   2005006067

*Our times cry out for a gospel-shaped spirituality
that is both intensely personal and
deeply aware of our suffering neighbor.*

Contents

૯

Foreword

UPPER ROOM MINISTRIES invited me to design a pilgrimage to South Africa. So in the fall of 2003 I returned to that country after a thirty-year absence. I traveled and met many dedicated Christians engaged in compassionate ministry. Everywhere I went I heard one name: Trevor Hudson. Then I was given a copy of his book, a copy that now has many highlighted passages and, like other much-loved books, is getting tattered on the edges. In the summer of 2004 I met Trevor in person at the SOULfeast Conference at Lake Junaluska, North Carolina. I immediately understood why people in South Africa hold him in such high esteem. Trevor, clearly a disciple of the living Christ and a man of prayer, speaks with a prophetic voice today. He urges us all to proclaim Jesus' message of good news to the poor, liberty to captives, and sight to the blind; to remember that we can only be true disciples if we give priority to prayer and holy listening.

Often we meet dedicated Christians who are simply worn out by the struggle to serve Christ in places of staggering need. Like my copy of Trevor's book they become tattered on the edges—too tired to pray, play, or take care of themselves.

Others of us see our primary ministry as prayer: we remain faithful to our daily discipline of time alone with God; we read books about prayer, go to prayer meetings, and schedule retreats for ourselves. But prayer can actually become the way we avoid taking action or even noticing the desperate needs of many among whom we live and work. In this book Trevor Hudson repeatedly calls us to be people of prayer who learn to listen to the neighbor, the forgotten and oppressed folk in our midst. Only then may we become agents of God's love and action through compassionate caring.

All of us journey day by day with Christ through the Spirit but sometimes we forget Divine Presence who walks beside us. We are all on pilgrimage; every experience, interaction, or roadblock we encounter can become a grace-filled opportunity to respond with loving obedience to the gospel. But we need to pay attention to our experience and willingly reflect upon our journey. The pilgrimages of pain and hope begun in the Johannesburg church that Trevor Hudson pastored require a lengthy preparatory period. Pilgrims learn that encounter, reflection, and transformation take place through the discipline of learning to be present to where they are, who they meet, and what they see as they go about their daily tasks. The seventeenth-century French writer Jeanne Pierre de Caussade coined the phrase "the sacrament of the present moment" to make clear that even the most ordinary experiences have profound meaning if we pay attention to them.

The practice of attentive presence is not easy however; it requires discipline. During The Upper Room Pilgrimage to South Africa many of us felt overwhelmed by the beauty, need, pain, and hope—both of the country and of those we met. Each day presented new challenges as well as blessings, but three practices enabled us to reflect on our experience: keeping a pilgrimage journal, sharing our experiences with one another, and taking time for silent reflection. At the end of the pilgrimage we created a corporate journal that deepened my insights as I read what others had said.

Trevor Hudson names these same essentials in his book and sees them as necessary in our daily journey with God. Keeping a pilgrimage journal, he says, encourages perseverance in the practice of reflection and leads us to greater knowledge of self. Honoring our need for regular times of solitude and silence around scripture and holy listening attunes us to the "still small voice." Creating opportunities to share our reflections with others expands and deepens our own understanding, while providing support and encouragement.

As I read this book I learned a new phrase for an old problem: *compassion fatigue*. Some of the wisest counsel in this book addresses my tendency to respond indiscriminately to perceived needs and then to find myself mired in exhausted resentment. Exhaustion is the thief of laughter and joy, and I lose the balance between celebration and responsibility. Is there any answer to this conundrum? Trevor responds to my question in practical terms: In order to walk with others in their need I must first become a compassionate neighbor to myself by taking care of my body, giving time to activities I enjoy, and processing my own pain. I may need to curb tendencies toward compulsive caring by not immediately responding to another's pain and by setting limits on my readiness to help. And, perhaps most difficult of all, I need to allow others to care for me. I sense that this gentle yet firm wisdom is offered by one who has struggled with the demands of being a faithful pastor and justice-builder, who gives voice to the prophetic truth of the gospel while seeking to honor the priority of contemplative prayer.

℮⌒

On my return to South Africa, my first visit since the end of apartheid, I discovered signs of hope and fell in love again with the country and its people. A vibrant, primal energy pulses in the drumming and dancing of those who know their deep connection with the soil of Africa. The interweaving of many groups, formerly separated by a pro-white government, was especially heartwarming at the first *Sedibeng* that The Upper Room sponsored in Johannesburg. *Sedibeng* means "to gather at the well" and reflects the traditional meeting place of native peoples in villages throughout Africa. We gathered together and drank deeply from the well of Christ's all-inclusive love. We marveled at the miracle wrought by the Truth and Reconciliation Commission which, instead of exacting the penalties deserved by former oppressors, torturers, and murderers, offered amnesty to those willing to own their crimes and ask for forgiveness. We witnessed the long lines of people waiting to vote in the election that marked ten years of freedom, and we learned that some had traveled for days on foot to exercise their right as citizens to participate in their own government. Signs of hope were everywhere.

Sadly, there is also much evidence of pain in the new South Africa. The poor remain poor and crime grows, especially in the larger cities where those without employment turn to theft. The AIDS pandemic continues to claim thousands of lives, and many myths about the disease add additional hurt to the pain of the disease itself. In the informal settlements, many barely survive in the lean-to shacks where they lack access to clean water and nutritious food. The government does not provide free education or the required school uniforms so, although education is open to all, many cannot afford it; and the cycle of impoverishment grows. At the same time the growth of multimillion-dollar houses and amenities is staggering, especially in the prime real estate locations by the ocean. The widening gap between rich and poor reflects the experience of the prophet Amos when he took his employer's goods to sell in the marketplace at Jerusalem. We in the developed nations and those whose wealth is gouged from the backs of the poor in South Africa would do well to listen to God's words addressed to Israel:

> They sell the righteous for silver,
>   and the needy for a pair of sandals—
> they . . . trample the head of the poor
> into the dust of the earth,
> and push the afflicted out of the way. . . .
> I hate, I despise your festivals
> and take no delight in your solemn assemblies. . . .
> Let justice roll down like waters,
> and righteousness like an ever-flowing stream.
> —Amos 2:6-7; 5:21, 24

In this context Trevor Hudson continues his ministry of compassion and his proclamation of Jesus' message of good news to the poor. His book does not offer consolation to the complacent or deny the reality of pain in the midst of joyous hope. *A Mile in My Shoes* is no simple "how-to" publication but, rather, a challenging imperative to pay attention to all around us and to engage in the spiritual disciplines that enable us to see, hear, and respond to the living Christ in our midst. My brief encounter with the author and repeated reflection on his book cause me to give grateful thanks for the integrity of Trevor's life and ministry. I long to embody such caring compassion and integrity in my own daily pilgrimage of pain and hope.

—*Elizabeth Canham*
December 30, 2004

Acknowledgments

MANY PEOPLE encouraged me as this book gradually came to life. My deep thanks go to the following:

- to David Wavre and Joyce Huggett for their gentle insistence that the pilgrimage experience was worth writing about;
- to Bill Meaker who corrected my grammar and made numerous helpful suggestions;
- to the pilgrims themselves, especially Stephen Carpenter, Brian Burger, Neil and Adele Thomas, and Gavin Launders for allowing me to quote their reflections;
- to Ruth Rice for her listening companionship on my own personal pilgrimage;
- to the Sisters at St. Benedict's, Rosettenville, and Sister Margaret Magdalen for their faithful intercessions and supportive interest in the book;
- to Lyn Meyer for placing her computer skills so generously at the service of this book;
- and lastly, to Debbie, Joni, and Mark who keep loving me through thick and thin. I dedicate the book to them.

Chapter 1

Introducing the Pilgrimage Experience

e⁓

I REMEMBER the exact moment the idea of a Pilgrimage of Pain and Hope was born. It was a Sunday afternoon in the bitterly cold August of 1982, and I was driving home from visiting Soweto with three overseas friends. Together we had attended a small meeting where Jean Vanier, founder of the extraordinary L'Arche movement, had met with a few people with handicapping conditions and their families. For almost three hours I had listened quietly to the life stories of ordinary men and women who lived amid crushing deprivation and oppression.

As I steered my car along the busy highway that linked Soweto to neighboring Johannesburg, their words and faces kept crossing my mind. Suddenly a thought came into my mind with surprising forcefulness and clarity: *Take members of your congregation with you to where their brothers and sisters are suffering* were the simple words that typed themselves across the screen of my mind. I pastored a largely middle-class suburban congregation safely shielded from the traumatized apartheid context of the early eighties in South Africa. Forced removals, poverty, and homelessness were abstractions in the experience of my congregation, as they were in my own. Few of us had ever consciously related our Christ-following to these social realities or experienced the sharing of life with and learning from those who knew firsthand the pain of these social contexts. Perhaps intentionally exposing ourselves to the suffering of others would change us and help us respond in appropriate ways.

I began to pray and plan. Ever since my own beginnings as a disciple of Jesus, I had been struck by the fact that many of the most Christlike spiritual leaders were men and women who lived in close relationship with those who suffered. People like Dorothy Day, Jean Vanier, Henri Nouwen, Cicely Saunders, Jackie Pullinger, Desmond Tutu were all pilgrims whose words and witness had greatly shaped my understanding of the Christ-following life. Through all these lives ran the common thread of a connection with the poor, the hurting, the broken, and the marginalized. *Could this be one reason why,* I wondered, *the transformative grace and caring compassion of Christ seemed so evident in their lives?* Could it be that if small groups from my local congregation were to spend time with those who suffered, we would also experience a similar conversion of our hearts and lives?

With these questions percolating in my mind, the idea of a Pilgrimage of Pain and Hope began to take form. I contacted friends and colleagues who ministered in possible pilgrimage sites and raised the question of a small group coming to spend time with them. They responded honestly with their concerns and suggestions: we would come as pilgrims, not as tourists; as learners, not as teachers; as receivers, not as givers; as listeners, not as talkers. Aware that much preparation would be needed to foster an appropriate pilgrim attitude among us, I sounded the call for our first pilgrimage experience and waited. Fourteen members of the congregation indicated an interest in becoming pilgrims. The adventure had begun.

Eight months later, after much careful preparation and planning, the first Pilgrimage of Pain and Hope was launched. Fifteen pilgrims, ranging in age from seventeen to midthirties, left the Kempton Park Methodist Church for an eight-day immersion into the struggles and joys of our suffering neighbors. I doubt that any of us realized the extent to which our journey together would impact our lives. Suffice to say that, upon returning home, I made a threefold resolve: (1) I would plan for our congregation an annual, weeklong Pilgrimage of Pain and Hope; (2) as best as I could in the light of the Christian tradition, I would keep trying to shape the pilgrimage experience into an effective means of spiritual formation; and (3) at a personal level I would seek to become a pilgrim in daily life. On the following pages I share insights and learnings that have become clearer as I have walked along the pilgrimage road. As I do this, I pray that the Spirit will call other Christ-followers to embrace the pilgrimage experience.

Essential Pilgrimage Ingredients

For almost a decade, the Pilgrimage of Pain and Hope was an integral part of our congregation's life. More than one hundred young and not-so-young adults participated. For many of these people the pilgrimage became an instrument of lasting personal transformation that led to profound changes in outlook and lifestyle. Repeatedly the pilgrims' lives bore clear evidence of ever-deepening commitment to the way of Christ. As our congregation's pilgrimage experience developed over the years and I began sharing the ideas with other congregations, it became clear that the concept rested upon three essential ingredients: *Encounter—Reflection—Transformation.* I will explore each aspect more fully in later chapters, but I want to introduce them briefly now.

ENCOUNTER

First, the Pilgrimage of Pain and Hope is a personal encounter with the pain of our shattered and fragmented societies. The South African pilgrimage experience encompassed several different suffering contexts: from informal housing settlements in desperately impoverished areas to shelters for the homeless and homes for those with mentally handicapping conditions to drug rehabilitation centers where young people struggled to break free of addiction. I planned no more than one exposure every few days so the various pilgrim groups could actually live with those they visited, put names to faces, and talk face to face with their hosts. I chose encounters that would specifically challenge any superficial response in possible gospel ministry.

Alongside this encounter with pain in the pilgrimage experience comes an encounter with hope. Throughout these deprived communities we discover those who resiliently refuse to become prisoners of helplessness and despair. Often unsung and anonymous, these hidden saints bring rays of faith, hope, and love to the lives they touch. Moreover, small bands of ministering Christ-followers often reside among those who suffer and hurt They seek to respond and act in faithful and obedient ways. Encountering these signs of hope challenges the pilgrims to examine their own faith responses within their lives and communities. They see hope resident in the future and acknowledge the creative difference their lives can make in a land torn by division and suffering. Things do not have to stay as they are. A church poster once proclaimed, "Christ has taken the inevitability out of history."

REFLECTION

Second, reflection on experience constitutes the next ingredient in the pilgrimage process. The pilgrims experience daily a wide range of emotions, circumstances, and people. Without reflection they run the risk of losing the transforming insights. Hence, throughout the pilgrimage, the participants receive the necessary space to reflect upon what is happening within and around them. Integral to this reflection process is their daily meditation upon the scriptures in light of the pilgrimage encounters. Writing out these reflections enables the pilgrims to express their feelings, clarify the issues with which they are wrestling, and articulate their desires for future actions of kingdom obedience.

TRANSFORMATION

While it is possible to plan into the pilgrimage experience the elements of encounter and reflection, the third ingredient cannot be ensured: transformation. Transformation into greater Christlikeness comes as a gift to those generously open to the Holy Spirit. Hearts of stone become hearts of flesh. Reflecting upon this evidence of changed hearts and lives among the pilgrims, I have written:

> The implanted seed of divine compassion begins to flower. Non-sentimental and caring deeds are birthed. Courage is given to speak truth to those principalities and powers intent on destroying the lives of people. Our hearts begin yearning for a society where there is justice and compassion for all. That this can begin to happen in our lives is the testimony of our pilgrims.[1]

PILGRIMS IN DAILY LIFE

Not every Christ-follower can go away on an eight-day pilgrimage. As the pilgrims returned home and shared their stories, many who listened expressed their disappointment that family and work responsibilities precluded their participation in this annual event. As I thought through this aspect I began to see that these three essential ingredients, *Encounter—Reflection—Transformation*, represent three critical movements of the authentic Christ-following life. As Jesus' disciples we are called into an ongoing engagement with our suffering neighbor, continued reflection upon our lives in the light of scripture, and a never-ending process of growing into Christlikeness. In other words, Christ-followers need to find a practical way of making the pilgrimage experience part of their daily lives.

Wrestling with this question of how whose who could not go away on a pilgrimage could become everyday pilgrims heralded another crucial discovery. Alongside the usual activities of solitude and silence, prayer and fasting, Bible study and meditation, I began to see the possibilities of the pilgrimage experience as a regular spiritual discipline undergirding our daily walk with God. Thus, from the pulpit and in pastoral conversations, I began sharing the idea of building these three pilgrimage ingredients into our everyday lives in a deliberate, conscious, and intentional manner. Many responded positively. Again I was astonished to witness how, when we give ourselves faithfully to this pilgrimage discipline, the Spirit of God transforms us into more compassionate and concerned people.

I do not write these words about everyday pilgrimage as a detached and clinical observer. At the time of writing I have not been in a position to lead an eight-day pilgrimage experience for almost six years. Increasing family commitments and change in local church environment, together with a different ministry job description, have diverted my energy and time in other directions. At first I felt that these changes would separate my spiritual journey from the human cries in my midst. However, as I have forged the three essential pilgrimage components into my overall life pattern, I feel that my practice of the pilgrimage experience has deepened. Indeed, I have come to see myself as a pilgrim in daily life. Everyday pilgrims seek to cultivate a particular attitude toward life—an attitude that sees the living Christ present in all things, especially in our encounters with those who suffer.

CONTEMPORARY RELEVANCE

We live in a day and age characterized by an unprecedented upsurge of spiritual searching. This widespread interest calls for careful discernment. On the one hand, the contemporary church has been inundated by various spiritualities that obsessively focus on inner matters yet reflect minimal concern for those who suffer. On the other hand, the church often endorses a spirituality of social struggle and liberation that sidesteps the biblical imperative for personal conversion and transformation. Such endorsement falls prey to the dangerous illusion that we can build a just and compassionate society while we remain the same. Indeed, our times cry out for a gospel-shaped spirituality that is both intensely personal and deeply aware of suffering neighbor.

Significantly, this desperate need for a more balanced spirituality coincides with the overall goal of the authentic Christ-following life, which involves our gradual inner transformation into greater Christlikeness. As disciples of Jesus we are called to live as he would if he were in our place. Whatever else this may mean, it involves learning how to become a more caring and compassionate person. Compassionate caring, as Paul's magnificent thirteenth chapter of First Corinthians points out, is *the* distinguishing mark of faithful discipleship. Compassionate caring creatively balances the inward-outward dynamic so characteristic of Jesus' life, saves us from falling prey to the latest fad in the spiritual supermarket, and catapults our lives into a deeper engagement with the brokenness of our world.

While the Spirit enables us to care the way Jesus did, this inward transformation of our hearts requires disciplined effort and planned cooperation. We seldom become more compassionate without working at it. Compassion usually comes as a grace-soaked gift to those who intentionally, consciously, and regularly place themselves before God. As noted, one practical way to cultivate compassion involves building the pilgrimage experience into our lives. Whether we embark upon an annual Pilgrimage of Pain and Hope or seek deliberately to become a pilgrim in daily life, we discover that the crucified and risen Christ meets us in the lives of those who suffer. Seldom does this encounter leave us as we are. For this reason, the relevance of the pilgrimage experience for our contemporary situation cannot be overemphasized.

In closing this introductory chapter, I must make it clear that I am a beginner when it comes to the life of compassion. Others do not always experience me as a caring person. Often I have been deaf to the human cries around me, blind to those in desperate need, and indifferent to those structures that hurt and harm God's people. Sometimes I do not even like those with whom I am bound together in Christ. Occasionally those closest to me have felt unappreciated, unnoticed, and unloved. Without doubt my greatest shortcomings have come through failures in loving. Yet in spite of my inadequacies, when it comes to the compassionate life and my limited understanding of what it means to be a concerned Christ-follower in our suffering world, I have been enriched enormously by the pilgrimage experience. I would be remiss not to share what I have been graciously given by those who suffer deeply.

INVITATION TO PILGRIMAGE

(The set of reflective questions that follow each chapter may be used for individuals or small-group settings.)

1. Introduce yourself to the group, sharing one aspect of your life that is going well at the moment.

2. Describe *one* experience in which another person's great suffering enriched and challenged your life.

3. How do you respond to the concept of a Pilgrimage of Pain and Hope?

4. How would you describe your present spiritual practice?
    • Nonexistent
    • Inward but lacking the outward dimension
    • Outward but lacking the inward dimension
    • Balanced

5. How do you feel about becoming a pilgrim in daily life?

Chapter 2

Preparing for Pilgrimage

A s I began planning our first Pilgrimage of Pain and Hope, I contacted several people around the country to check out our intentions. One particular phone call, made to a good friend living and ministering in an impoverished rural settlement, exercised a significant influence upon our preparations. After explaining at some length the purpose of our intended pilgrimage and telling her a little about those traveling with me, I asked whether she would be prepared to coordinate our visit from her end. After a few moments of silence, as if she were trying to find the right words, her words communicated both encouragement and challenge. "I'm sure the community will welcome you warmly, but," she paused briefly and then added, "please ensure that you come as pilgrims and not as tourists on a sightseeing tour."

I thought about my friend's words. Spoken with firm conviction and wise concern they boldly underlined the necessity of suitable preparation. We pilgrims were not about to visit sacred shrines or religious venues of historical interest but rather tiptoe upon the holy ground of other people's suffering. While the pilgrimage would require physical preparation, including decisions about itinerary, routes, means of travel, arrangements with hosts, and finances, our top priority became the cultivation of an appropriate pilgrim attitude.

My friend's words apply to our everyday lives as Christ-followers as well. The gospel call invites us to apprentice ourselves to Jesus, become pilgrims along the compassionate way, and journey deeper together into the heart and life of God. In our contemporary setting, however, Christians often look more like bustling tourists then faithful pilgrims patiently engaged upon an eternal pilgrimage into Divine Love. Countless people today make periodic excursions into the spiritual supermarket in pursuit of a novel offer, but few seem willing to sign up as pilgrims in the lifelong adventure of discipleship. Eugene Peterson describes perceptively the situation in which we find ourselves:

> Religion in our time has been captured by the tourist mindset. Religion is understood as a visit to an attractive site to be made when we have adequate leisure. For some it is a weekly jaunt to church. For others, occasional visits to special services. Some, with a bent for religious entertainment and sacred diversion, plan their lives around special events like retreats, rallies and conferences. We go to see a new personality, to hear a new truth, to get a new experience and so, somehow, expand our otherwise humdrum lives.[1]

How, then, do we go about cultivating a pilgrim attitude? Applicable to every apprentice pilgrim, whether embarking upon a planned pilgrimage experience or not, this question deserves careful attention. Otherwise our lives run the risk of becoming characterized by aimless drifting, smug self-concern, and bland superficiality. Based upon the biblical witness, insights from mentors, and my personal experience with the Pilgrimage of Pain and Hope, I will outline three interwoven ingredients of a pilgrim posture. I will also suggest some practical ways through which we can begin forging them into our everyday lives. These three ingredients are

- learning to be present,
- learning to listen,
- learning to notice.

LEARNING TO BE PRESENT

I learned the word *present* in my first year at primary school, though it would be many years before I discovered some of its rich meanings. I can still remember sitting in my kindergarten classroom while the teacher took attendance. As she called out the names, each of us answered "present." Even if half asleep, preoccupied with playmates for break, or daydreaming about the sports match after school, I would automatically say "present" when she called my name. Then I little realized that I was often far from being present at all. There had taken place, to use an arresting phrase from the writings of Douglas Steere, an "interior emigration" of my mind and heart from the living moment.[2]

We experience this interior emigration in daily life. Our distracted, frantic, and hurried lifestyles can keep us from being truly present to those around us. I'm sure that, without too much effort, you can think of a recent encounter when you were not really "all there" for the other person. I had this experience as I wrote this chapter. I had just picked up my son from school, and he was sharing excitedly some news about a forthcoming soccer match in which he would play. My mind, however, was preoccupied with a commitment I had that afternoon. Sensing my total absence from the present moment, my son suddenly said, "Dad, tell me what I have just said." I couldn't. And in that moment I felt again the aching sadness of not being present to those I love most.

One heart-wrenching Gospel encounter takes place when the disciples fail to be present to Jesus in his time of deep need. Recall briefly that scene of betrayal and dereliction: the night before the crucifixion drama Jesus retreats with his friends to the Gethsemane garden. Aware of the rapidly approaching ordeal, Jesus faces a time of intense spiritual preparation, rigorous heart searching, and profound anguish of soul. Before leaving the disciples to pray alone, Jesus asks his companions to be with him, to sit near him, and to stay awake. Three times they let him down by dozing off and not being present where they are. Can you imagine the pain in Jesus' heart when he keeps finding them asleep. (See Mark 14:32-42.) Might the crucified and risen Christ, as he meets us in those who suffer today, continue to be in pain because of our failure to be present?

Let me describe what it means to be truly present. Being present involves letting go of our constant preoccupations, immersing ourselves in the here and now, and giving ourselves wholeheartedly to whatever is at hand. Involving far more than being merely physically present, it's about becoming more aware, alert, awake to the full-ness of the immediate moment. If we are with another person, it means engaging him or her with all of our heart, our mind, our soul, and our strength. Such whole-hearted attention requires patience, time, and disciplined effort. And it is one of the greatest gifts that we can give to those around us, especially our suffering neighbor. When a priest asked the Russian spiritual writer Catherine de Hueck Doherty what contribution he could make to a hurting and broken world, she answered simply, "Your presence, Father."[3]

Pilgrims seek to be truly present where they are. By focusing fully on all that the present moment holds, they indicate their willingness to be influenced, perhaps even transformed, by their everyday and commonplace expe-riences. Their posture before the mystery of life is one of vulnerable openness, nonpossessive engagement, rever-ent participation, and childlike wonder. In these respects their mind-set differs vastly from that of tourists who, as they drift from one place of interest to another, mainly seek to derive whatever pleasure they can. Given the widespread prevalence throughout the Western world of this tourist mentality toward life and its infiltration into much current spirituality, developing a pilgrim mental-ity usually begins with a conscious choice to learn how to be present: "Dear Lord, show me how to open my life more generously to the meaning and mystery of the present moment."

To develop a more present-minded way of living, you might experiment regularly with an exercise that I first came across in the writings of Metropolitan Antony.[4] The basic steps go as follows: Set aside some time, perhaps five minutes, to do nothing. Simply sit down in your room and say, "I am seated; I am doing nothing. I will do nothing for the next five minutes." Having declared your intention for this little space of time, decide firmly that nothing will pull you away during these five minutes. If you find yourself emigrating mentally into the past or the future, bring yourself back to the here and now with the thought, *I am here in the presence of God, in my own presence, and in the presence of all the furniture that is around me, just still, moving nowhere.* I have discovered that doing this exercise regularly builds up the capacity to live more deeply in the present within our everyday lives.

LEARNING TO LISTEN

Listening is the second essential component of the pilgrim attitude. Compassion, as we have already seen, lies at the heart of the spiritual journey. We grow toward Christlikeness only as we become more caring. A noncaring Christ-follower is a contradiction in terms. However, we cannot show real concern, especially for those in pain, unless we first take time to listen. We can only love those to whom we genuinely listen. For this reason, if we intend to put our lives alongside those who suffer and reflect to them the compassion of Christ, our presence must always be a listening one. This could be why James, one of the first spiritual mentors in the early church, encouraged his readers to "be quick to listen, slow to speak" (James 1:19).

Christians are not well known for their listening. Some years ago, I had an experience that presses home this observation. My family and I strolled along a Johannesburg street and suddenly found ourselves surrounded by a group of enthusiastic Christians. Armed with tracts and Bibles they stopped us in our tracks to proclaim the facts of the gospel. As they spoke about Jesus and urged us to accept him into our lives, I tried vainly to get a word in. All I wanted to say was, "Folks, we're on the same side as you," but they would not give me a chance. Even though they were physically present with us, they failed to communicate the compassionate heart of the Divine Pilgrim. At no stage did they attempt to find out who and where we were before presenting us with the claims of Christ. In their failure to take seriously James's injunction about listening, their actions contradicted the message of God's grace and love.

We need not judge this group of zealous Christians. Often our own inability to listen well has made others feel isolated, unaccepted, and unloved. Thankfully, we can all learn to listen better. While a few people seem naturally gifted as listeners, most of us need to develop this vital gateway to compassion. Cultivating a listening life, however, does not occur overnight. Few activities require as much energy, effort, and patience. Involving at least three basic steps, good listening enables us to grow in the compassionate Way, becoming more faithful pilgrims at heart.

1. *Stop talking.*

If we want to learn to listen we must stop talking. We cannot speak and listen at the same time. Failure to grasp this common-sense reality impedes many from making any significant progress in the listening life. Unless we bridle our tongues, stop our constant chatter, and check our tendencies to interrupt others as they speak, we cannot truly listen to another. Restricting our speech in these ways does not come easily. Deeply ingrained into the tongue are talkative habits that resist determinedly any kind of change. The fact that this member of the body seems to possess a life of its own means that our desire to be listening pilgrims requires that we discipline ourselves firmly. Practicing the silence of not speaking in situations that invite our compassionate presence, begins the listening journey.

2. *Give total attention to the one speaking.*

Learning to listen involves giving our total attention to the person speaking. Merely being silent does not ensure that we are really listening. We could be dead, asleep, daydreaming, or totally preoccupied with our own thoughts and feelings. We've all experienced speaking to someone whose vacant eyes and faraway look indicate that he or she has not heard a word. By contrast, true listeners concentrate intently upon the speaker's words, the feelings that accompany the words, and the silences between them. Such concentration communicates nonverbally a genuine and positive interest in what they are hearing. Morton Kelsey captures this dynamic element of the listening process when he writes, "Real listening is being silent with another person or group of persons in an active way."[5]

3. *Communicate understanding of what is shared.*

Good listeners try to communicate their understanding of what persons share with them. They don't *always* remain silent. Whenever appropriate they try to clarify what they hear the other person saying. Like any other communication skill, this reflective listening style can be misused and become a mechanical counterfeit of the real thing. Nonetheless, the person speaking will feel listened to if we indicate some grasp of what is being said. During my training for pastoral ministry, one of my tutors would constantly say to me, "Trevor, the most healing gift that you can give to someone in pain is the awareness that you are honestly trying to understand what they are going through, even if you get it wrong."

Against the background of these basic guidelines I invite you to assess the quality of your current listening ability. Growing in self-awareness about our listening ability often initiates a fresh commitment to become a better listener. Here are ten straightforward yes or no questions to consider. A positive answer to any number of them could challenge you to develop more consciously a listening heart.

- Am I known as a chatterbox?
- Do I interrupt others in midsentence?
- Do I "switch off" when I disagree with what's being said?
- Do I complete other people's sentences?
- During conversations am I often preoccupied with my own thoughts and feelings?
- Do I plan my answer while others speak?
- Do I fear silence in conversations?
- Do I tend to jump in with my own story and take over instead of listening?
- Am I often impatient while listening?
- Do those closest to me often complain that I don't listen to them?

Learning to Notice

Christ-followers live in the faith that the Divine Presence interpenetrates all of our lives. Apostle Paul witnesses to this startling reality when, in his message to the Athenians, he declares boldly that God is always near, for "in him we live and move and have our being" (Acts 17:28). The writer of Ephesians brings this conviction into even sharper focus when he writes that there is "one God and Father of all, who is above all and through all and in all" (Eph. 4:6). Whether we acknowledge it or not, the Holy One enfolds each of our lives, pours out continuously divine love upon us, and communicates constantly with us. Wherever we stand—in the kitchen or the workplace—is holy ground. Jesus said to his disciples in the closing moments of his earthly ministry, "And remember, I am with you always, to the end of the age" (Matt. 28:20).

While the Holy encounters us wherever we are, God meets us especially in our interactions with those who suffer. We learn this from Jesus himself who, as God come in the flesh, identifies himself deeply with suffering men and women. From the outset of his public ministry he fosters an intimate connection with the broken and hurting. He touches the leper, befriends the outcast, delivers the oppressed, welcomes the sinner, and forgives the guilty. On the cross he takes a radical step by identifying himself totally with every sinned-against human being. In his cry, "My God, my God, why have you forsaken me?" (Mark 15:34), he becomes one with all who feel devastated, abandoned, and cut off from God in their suffering. His total connection with those in pain leads him to say to his disciples: "Truly I tell you, just as you did it to one of the least of these who are members of my family, you did it to me" (Matt. 25:40).

If God comes so close to us in our everyday experiences and encounters, we must learn how to notice the Divine Presence. Discerning what God is doing and saying in our midst lays the foundations for the faithful pilgrim's responses. I learned this from my first "formal" spiritual director back in 1978. Once a month we would meet together and reflect upon my pilgrimage with Christ. Our times together tended to follow a strikingly similar pattern. Usually I began by telling her the events and experience of my life over the past few weeks. Besides talking about my experiences of prayer and meditation upon the scriptures, I would speak also about how things were going at work, my relationships at home and with friends, as well as my involvement with those living in painful situations. After I had finished, my soul-friend would often ask an intriguing question, "I wonder where God is active in all of this?"

This simple question reminded me of the biblical truth that I could encounter God everywhere and in anything. Looking back to the beginnings of my walk with Christ, I realize that I lived in a state of inner segregation. I tended to separate my life into two distinct compartments: the spiritual and the nonspiritual. Into the former I placed activities like going to church, attending fellowship groups, reading the Bible, and witnessing; the rest of my life's activities comprised the latter. This division led to splits in my spiritual journey between the sacred and the secular, the material and the spiritual, the visible and the invisible, and eventually between God and most of my life. Perhaps sensing this, my spiritual director gently fostered a new attitude within me, an attitude that would help me learn to notice the reality and experience of God in all things.

But my spiritual director did more than merely raise a question about the whereabouts of God's presence. In our conversations she would encourage me to be attentive to my inner responses to my lived experiences. By helping me express these thoughts and feelings and reflect on them, she slowly taught me how to discern the Divine Whisper. While God speaks in many ways through creation, interactions with others, the preaching and teaching of the church, the cry of our suffering neighbor and, most importantly, through our meditation upon scripture—the inward effect of being addressed usually takes the shape of a distinctive thought or feeling.

These movements of heart and mind are the way God speaks to us; they are the quiet sounds of God's still small voice. Noticing them draws us deeper into God's heart, sensitizes our hearts to the promptings of the Spirit, and guides our steps along the pilgrimage road.

Two heartbroken Emmaus pilgrims return home from Jerusalem after the crucifixion. As they trudge along the road after the fateful events of that first Good Friday Jesus joins them in a form that they do not immediately recognize. When he asks about their conversation, the story flows out. They tell him that their leader, whom they had hoped would liberate Israel, had been sentenced to death and crucified. Moreover, three days later some women had gone to his tomb only to find it empty.

At first Jesus listens attentively and then, almost rudely, interrupts the two travelers and begins to explain from the scriptures about the Messiah's suffering. As he speaks, his words affect the pilgrims inwardly. Later, their reflections upon these inner responses confirm the identity of the stranger as the risen Jesus. They say to each other, "Were not our *hearts* burning within us while he was talking to us on the road?" (Luke 24:32, my italics).

How do we nurture the pilgrim mentality of noticing what God is doing and saying within our lives? Allow me to describe a simple exercise that helps us begin: take a sheet of paper, or a journal if you use one, and list randomly the experiences and encounters of the last twenty-four hours. Next to each item jot down your thoughts and feelings about it. Reflect prayerfully upon these affective responses, these inner movements of heart and mind, and ask the Spirit of God to draw your attention to the Divine Whisper. Certain key questions may facilitate this discernment process:

- Which draw me in the direction of a fuller and more creative life?

- How am I being invited into a closer walk with God; a greater openness towards others; a deeper regard for myself?

- In what ways am I being attracted toward a life more expressive of Jesus' compassionate spirit?

Amidst the numerous responses and reactions that jostle around inside our lives, these three questions assist us to notice those gentle inner nudges through which God may be seeking to lead us into greater fullness of life.[6]

To this day I remain thankful for those words spoken by my friend before our first Pilgrimage of Pain and Hope. They remind us that, if we ever choose to enter the world of another person's suffering, we must cultivate a genuine pilgrim attitude. Being present roots the relationship with our hurting neighbor in the reality of the here-and-now moment. Listening to his or her human cry communicates our presence as a caring and compassionate one. Noticing the Divine Presence at the heart of the suffering opens our inner eyes and ears to what God may be doing and saying. Should we therefore decide to embrace the pilgrimage experience and build its ingredients into our everyday lives, this never-ceasing preparation of the heart is crucial.

INVITATION TO PILGRIMAGE

1. Under the headings *tourist* and *pilgrim* make two columns on a sheet of paper. Brainstorm your immediate responses to these two words. Compare the two lists, and notice their similarities and differences.

2. How do you sometimes experience an "interior emigration" from the present moment?

3. Share your response to the quick quiz (page 35) on your listening style.

4. Share *one* way in which you experience the divine presence in your everyday life.

5. In what *one* way do you desire to cultivate a genuine pilgrim attitude toward life?

Chapter 3

Encountering Our Suffering Neighbor

℮⁓

F OR OVER twenty-five years I have pursued the call of being a pastor. This daily work includes the daunting responsibility of enabling others to grow as disciples of Jesus. In responding to this vocational challenge I lead Bible studies, host silent retreats, offer spiritual counsel, conduct teaching seminars, participate in small groups, and engage in countless pastoral conversations. While all these ministry endeavors are definitely worthwhile, without the specific ingredients that the pilgrimage experience offers, these efforts at spiritual formation lack a vital ingredient. Arising from careful observation of the changed lives of those pilgrims who have opened themselves to their suffering neighbors, this conviction shapes significantly the way in which I now encourage others along the Christ-following path.

I encourage the pilgrimage experience as a method for personal transformation and change not only because of what I see in others' lives. In my personal experience, my suffering neighbor is where I meet the crucified and risen Christ. Each day I am given privileged access into the lives of persons who suffer greatly. These daily encounters with the terminally ill, the depressed, the economically poor, the retrenched, the divorced, the childless, the addicted, the elderly, the bereaved, and other suffering men and women affect profoundly my understanding and experience of the Christ-following life. The Spirit has used these relationships to foster my ongoing conversion.

Effective spiritual directors often encourage first-hand encounter with broken and hurting people. One case study that springs immediately to mind was the relationship between Baron Friedrich von Hugel and Evelyn Underhill. Evelyn grew up in a comfortable London home, married a successful lawyer, and gave her life to the study of the church's great mystics. In her midforties, while struggling with midlife despair, she approached the German Christian and asked him to be her spiritual guide. Through his counsel, given mainly in the form of written letters, he enabled her to discover a richer and more personal relationship with Jesus. He suggested that for her faith to descend from her head into her heart, she should have regular contact with the poor. In one letter he writes,

> I believe you ought to get yourself, gently and gradually, interested in the poor; that you should visit them, very quietly and unostentatiously, with as little incorporation as possible into Visiting Societies etc. You badly want de-intellectualizing or at least developing homely human sense and spirit dispositions. . . . I would carefully give preference to the two weekly visitations of the poor above anything else, excepting definite home and family duties.[1]

Unless we try to describe what happens in these exposure moments, our discussion about the value of the pilgrimage experience remains at the abstract level. Indeed, some feel that this structured form of contact lacks the spontaneity characteristic of heartfelt compassion and therefore is limited. Combining insights gleaned from the scriptures, wisdom gained from influential mentors, and lessons learned on the pilgrimages themselves, I believe that when we open our lives to those who suffer, three things happen. The Spirit of God

1. opens blind eyes,
2. uncovers inner poverty,
3. reveals hidden riches.

Such awareness and self-knowledge constitute crucial prerequisites for traveling down the conversion road. Allow me to elaborate briefly.

OPENING BLIND EYES

Has Jesus' emphasis on eyesight ever struck you? Not only does he heal people of physical blindness, but he invites his hearers to evaluate the quality of their own vision. (See Matthew 6:22; 7:3; Mark 8:23; John 4:35.) He believes strongly that the way we see others determines our behavior toward them. This appears to be the central thrust of his provocative parable about the Last Judgment, in which the Judge separates people from one another like sheep from goats. Those on the right are pronounced "blessed," while those on the left are sent away to fend for themselves. Notice that the criterion upon which the judgment takes place has to do with how much or how little each group has seen. In his comment upon this Gospel passage John Claypool observes:

Those on the right obviously had learned to utilize all their capacities of sight—the eyes of the body, of the mind, of the heart. And because of their complete sight, those people had been moved to respond to the sick, the hungry, the naked, the imprisoned, the outcast. They had seen beneath surface appearances to the Ultimate dimensions—where all persons are in God and God is in all persons.[2]

It's easy today not to recognize these sacred depths in our suffering neighbor, and the reasons for this blindness of heart vary. Constant media bombardment of human need often breeds a bland familiarity that generalizes suffering men and women into groups like the poor, the homeless, the unemployed, the elderly. Within these generalizations we lose sight of the spiritual dimensions present in each human being. Our anonymous encounters with beggars, street children, destitute men and women give rise to a sense of powerlessness that makes many of us look in another direction. Just yesterday I experienced this when I stopped at a traffic light. On the street corner stood a young mother with a crying baby strapped to her back. She held a card that asked for food or work. Almost automatically I avoided her eyes. I did not even want to acknowledge her presence, let alone see Christ in her.

We cannot meet all the needs that surround us, but tragic consequences flow from our failure to recognize the suffering neighbor for who he or she really is. These consequences range from a cold indifference to the human cries around us to cynicism and even resentment toward people's needs; a lack of engagement with those "principalities and powers" that crush and oppress—to a tragic loss of our own humanness. However (and this is one of the aims of the pilgrimage experience), when we share personally with those who suffer, put names to faces, listen to life stories, receive the gifts they offer, it creates a climate in which we learn to see differently. These personal encounters help pilgrims see the suffering neighbor as a brother or sister made in the image of God and in whom Christ dwells. Such recognition and awareness generates a new way of relating that makes genuine compassion possible.

Perhaps now we can understand better the conversation between a wise old spiritual master and his disciples. Once he asked them, "How can we know when the darkness is leaving and the dawn is coming?"

The disciples were quiet for a moment, and then one answered, "When we can see a tree in the distance and know that it is an elm and not a juniper." Another responded, "When we can see an animal, and know that it is a fox and not a wolf."

"No," said the old man, "those things will not help us."

Puzzled, the students asked, "How then can we know?"

The master leaned over and said to them quietly, "We know the darkness is leaving and the dawn is coming when we can see another person and know that this is our brother or our sister; for otherwise, no matter what time it is, it is still dark."[3]

It may help to reflect upon the health of your own eyesight. Several questions could guide this diagnostic exercise. They include the following:

- Is my seeing limited by the other person's color, class, or culture?

- Do I focus upon outward appearances in my dealings with people?
- Do I see people primarily as groups?
- Do I view others based on first impressions rather than hearing them out?
- Do I look at possessions as being more important than persons?

If you answer affirmatively to one or more of these questions, I invite you to pray a one-sentence prayer that I use often in my own personal devotions, "Lord Jesus, please help me to see each person whom I meet today as someone of infinite value and immense worth."

Uncovering Our Inner Poverty

One person whose life example and writings influence the underlying thinking of the Pilgrimage of Pain and Hope is Jean Vanier. In August 1964, Vanier bought a small house in Trosly Breuil, a small village to the north of Paris, and invited two men with handicapping conditions to share it with him. So began L'Arche (the Ark), an extraordinary movement where people who are often rejected and marginalized in today's success-bound world live together with "assistants." In these family-like communities the inhabitants get to know one another, learn to share joys and struggles, and help one another live more fully.

Today L'Arche homes around the world demonstrate an alternative way of caring for those with disabilities. But the real significance of the L'Arche movement goes deeper. As Jean Vanier learned and as his writings make clear, these encounters with suffering men and women uncover the poverty of our hearts.

Vanier's first two family members, Raphael and Philip, had both physical and mental handicaps. Raphael had a vocabulary of about twenty words and a very limited understanding, while Philip could only walk with a crutch. Sharing their lives on a daily basis plunged Vanier into a world of indescribable anguish that initiated a process of profound inner transformation within his own heart.

Hidden within the hearts of the two men was a deep desire for communion, friendship, and love. Yet these qualities of heart did not come easily to Vanier. He had been brought up to be efficient and productive, to intellectualize and compete. He experienced discomfort just being with people, let alone with people who could hardly speak or had little to speak about. Vanier describes his painful discovery of the hardness in his own heart:

> I discovered something which I had never confronted before, that there were immense forces of darkness and hatred within my own heart. At particular moments of fatigue or stress, I saw forces of hate rising up inside me, and the capacity to hurt someone who was weak and was provoking me! That, I think, was what caused me the most pain: to discover who I really am, and to realize that maybe I did not want to know who I really was! I did not want to admit all the garbage inside me.[4]

This honesty invites us to reflect thoughtfully on our own lives. Pause for a moment and ask yourself when you have experienced similar feelings in personal interactions with the hurt and broken. On the Pilgrimages of Pain and

Hope, pilgrims encountered the different worlds of suffering around them and spent time with those living there. Many of us had to confront the garbage in our own hearts. Ranging from feelings of indifference, anger, frustration, and superiority to deeply rooted prejudices toward others different in color and culture, we discovered that this inner brokenness often prevented genuine relationship. The desire to live a compassionate life required that we recognize and engage our own inner poverty.

This task is seldom easy. Facing our inner poverty means letting go of virtuous illusions about ourselves as guileless, respectable, and caring people. So, rather than acknowledge the garbage in our hearts, we pretend that all is well within. Or we try to escape our own ugliness by losing ourselves in frantic religious activity, *doing* things for those in need instead of entering into communion and friendship with them. Whatever shape the poverty of our hearts may take, our immediate response is usually to hide or ignore it.

Recently I addressed a women's group involved in valuable charity work. During my talk I suggested the importance of confessing the darker and more destructive sides of our personalities. Afterward one lady came up to the podium and said, "I don't understand what you are trying to get at. I love everyone I meet." Practically, how do we engage creatively our inner poverty?

1. *Acknowledge negative feelings and reactions.*

First and foremost, when negative feelings and reactions emerge in our dealings with suffering people, we can acknowledge those feelings. We cannot engage what we do not acknowledge. Then we can find a trusted friend, a spiritual companion, or a competent counselor with whom to share these darker aspects of ourselves. Few of us can face our interior darkness without the listening and nonjudgmental presence of another person.

After acknowledging the aggression, violence, and hatred that lurks inside, we can begin to take responsibility for what is there. As Christ-followers we affirm our goal to become more like him and express those aspects of our lives that lead us in this particular direction. Rarely does God change hearts without determined cooperation and disciplined effort. As Paul writes, "Keep on working with fear and trembling to complete your salvation, because God is always at work in you to make you willing and able to obey his own purpose" (Phil. 2:13, GNT).

2. Call out for God's help.

Second, we engage our inner poverty creatively by calling out for God's help. We cannot grow into greater Christ-likeness in our own strength, nor can we root out the dark forces of our hearts. Besides the support and care of trusted companions who bear with us in our wretchedness, we need power from beyond ourselves. A change needs to occur within us that we ourselves cannot bring about. Recognizing the impossibility of self-redemption, we cry out to God and ask for what we need. Then we discover that God meets us in our place of deepest brokenness, accepts us as we are, and offers us with crucified hands the gifts of grace and mercy. While this prayer encounter seldom expels completely the darkness within our hearts, it enables us to overcome our poverty within and keep moving toward our goal of becoming more compassionate followers of Christ.

On the Pilgrimages of Pain and Hope I adapt a favorite prayer exercise to help the pilgrims experience these two steps. You might try this meditation when, in interactions with suffering men and women, your own inner poverty confronts you.

Here is the basic outline:

Imagine yourself sitting quietly in the room of your heart. Its general state of untidiness and messiness represents your failure to connect compassionately with those who are hurt and broken. As you look around at the unmade bed, overflowing trash bin, the clothing lying around, the unwashed dishes piled high in the sink, you hear an accusing voice say, "You are useless when it comes to caring for others. Why don't you give up seeking to be a Christ-follower. You will never be an effective instrument of the divine love."

As you listen to these words from the accuser, you hear the sound of gentle, persistent knocking at the door. You get up from your chair, walk across the room, and open the door. Standing before you in the doorway is the figure of the crucified and risen Jesus, lantern in hand, the other hand raised to knock, a crown of thorns pressed into his head. He says, "Look at me. I stand at the door. I knock. If you hear me call and open the door, I'll come right in and sit down to supper with you" (Rev. 3:20, *The Message*).

As you open the door wider the ever-present Lord enters your room. The light from his lantern radiates warm rays of hope into the shabbiness around you. Together you sit down at the table upon which there is bread and wine. He asks you to tell him about the dark forces that rise up within you when you are with those who suffer. As you share your heart he listens with acceptance, understanding, and empathy. Then he takes a loaf of bread, breaks off a piece, and gives it to you with the words, "This is my body broken for you." He also takes a cup of wine, blesses it, and shares it with you, saying, "This is my blood shed for you." Before he gets up to leave, he places his hand upon your shoulder and says to you by name, "I will be with you even until the end. Receive now my love to go with you. Bring that love to others, especially to the suffering neighbor that my Father places upon your path. No matter how messy your life may be, I will never give up on you."[5]

REVEALING OUR HIDDEN RICHES

Some time ago I meditated on Jesus' well-known words, "This is my commandment, that you love one another as I have loved you" (John 15:12). These words usually leave me feeling like a failure when it comes to caring for those around me. This time as I turned this sentence over in my mind and thought about its possible meanings for my life, it struck me that Jesus actually believes in my capacity to love as he loves. It seemed as if he was saying to me through these words, "Trevor, tucked away in your depths are amazing capacities for loving. Know that you are as capable of loving others as I would if I were in your place. Allow my Spirit to reveal these hidden riches so you may express them and become the person God wants you to be."

Further reflection upon Jesus' commandment helped me understand life in a more hopeful and positive way.

We possess not only considerable inner garbage but also God-given resources for compassionate living. Biblical faith consistently asserts that created in the image and likeness of Love, we may learn to love as God does. (See Genesis 1:27; Ephesians 5:2; 1 John 4:16.) However, this capacity to love gets buried beneath our excessive egoism, our many self-centered choices, and our constant preoccupation with our own well-being. We become blind to our hidden riches, unaware of how much we can give to others and consequently fail to become who we are capable of becoming.

Our encounter with those who suffer reveals our hidden riches and helps us become our true selves. This revelation happens repeatedly in the lives of pilgrims on our Pilgrimages of Pain and Hope. As they open themselves to their suffering neighbor and enter into communion with him or her, their concealed compassionate natures begin to flower. This unfolding of who they truly are finds expression in various ways:

- egocentric attitudes and drives start being replaced by more caring responses;
- self-centeredness slowly gives way to a growing awareness of other people's needs; and
- in the place of obsessive self-interest, a concern for the common good develops.

These changes in the lives of the pilgrims show that interactions with suffering people can reveal not only what is worst about us *but also what is most beautiful.*

Our encounters with those who suffer reveal our hidden riches for three reasons. First, these encounters affect our hearts far more than they do our heads. Media images and statistics of human misery bombard us. Never before have we known so much about our world's brokenness. However, while we often discuss and debate what we see on the television or read in the newspapers, these media exposures seldom lead us toward greater compassion. But when painful realities assume a human face to whom we can put a name and to whose story we can listen, a meeting of human hearts takes place. Such heart encounters possess the power to uncover the more compassionate dimensions of our natures.

Second, when among people in pain—whether in a hospice for the dying, a home for persons with mentally handicapping conditions, a shelter for abused children, or a care center for the elderly—we discover that those present call forth the gifts that only our hearts can give. They do not so much need the skills of our hands or the knowledge of our minds as they do the compassion of our hearts. It is as if the suffering person extends an invitation to us saying, "Before you do anything for me, please come alongside me. Enter into communion with me so that you can be with me in my pain. Walk alongside me as my friend and companion." Deep treasures emerge from our hearts when we seek to respond to this cry for friendship, companionship, and solidarity.

Third, suffering people evoke the more compassionate sides of our personalities by demonstrating a remarkable capacity to extend themselves in generous caring. One pilgrimage experience stands out vividly in my memory.[6] Some years ago the pilgrims and I spent three days sharing life with a deprived and dispossessed community. Two of the pilgrims, both young women in their early twenties, lived with a family of six in a two-room dwelling. For the duration of their stay the husband and wife insisted that the two pilgrims use their bed while they themselves slept on the floor in the adjoining room with their children. Each morning they found that water had been heated for them over an open fire and a breakfast cooked. When they left, the family gave them a small gift to take back to their families.

Next we stayed in an exclusive and affluent suburb of a major South African city. The same two pilgrims were placed with a couple who lived alone in a two-story home. When they arrived, the young adults were asked to sleep on the carpet in the family room in sleeping bags. A domestic worker cooked their breakfast, which was left on the kitchen table and eaten without the company of their hosts. On the last day of their stay these pilgrims discovered upstairs three unused, furnished bedrooms. Their contrasting experience became for all on that pilgrimage a powerful demonstration of how our suffering neighbors, through their compassionate actions, can challenge us to express the hidden riches of our hearts.

In describing how the suffering neighbor can become God's catalyst in our ongoing conversion, I do not want to romanticize these encounters. Like ourselves, those who suffer are also sinful, fallible, and broken human beings. Nonetheless, when we enter into communion with someone in deep pain and anguish, we do not remain the same. The relationship can open our eyes, uncover our inner poverty, and reveal our hidden riches. For these reasons, intentional exposure to suffering neighbor warrants becoming a priority in the lives of serious Christ-followers. Otherwise, we may not grow into the compassionate and caring people that God wants us to be.

INVITATION TO PILGRIMAGE

1. What has helped you most to grow as a follower of Christ?

2. On the basis of the questionnaire on pages 45–46, how would you describe the health of your current eyesight?

3. Name *one* negative feeling that sometimes surfaces when you are with a suffering person?

4. How do you respond to your potential to love as Jesus loved?

5. Close your time of group sharing by taking part in the imaginative meditation outlined in this chapter (pages 50–51). It may help to have a group member prepare this meditation beforehand and lead the rest of the group through it.

Chapter 4

Reflecting upon
Our Experiences

 ❧

ONE SIMPLE SENTENCE, spoken to me by my first
pastoral supervisor, continues to exercise a powerful influence upon the way I work as a pastor. His words
shape considerably my present understanding of how we
can grow in awareness, deepen our spirituality, and forge
a more compassionate lifestyle. Each week during my initial year of pastoral ministry as we sat opposite each other
in his study reviewing my daily activities, he underlined
the importance of our time together by qualifying a com-
monly held assumption. "Always remember, Trevor," he
would say, "we do not learn from experience; we learn
from reflection upon experience."

Over the years I applied my mentor's counsel both to
my own faith journey and to my ministry efforts within
the local congregation. As I did so, I became firmly con-
vinced that, unless we value and practice reflection, little personal transformation occurs. Unreflected-upon
experience seldom yields its life-giving secrets. Too
many of us work and live without reflection, without
gaining any objective perspective on our behavior or any
understanding of why we do what we do. Think of how

often we make the same mistakes, repeat the same destructive behavioral patterns without ever pausing to look at what may be taking place in our lives. Only when we stop to reflect upon these experiences and extract their hidden insights do we open ourselves to the possibilities of real change.

Yesterday, while spending time with a dispirited youth worker, I witnessed again how reflection initiates new beginnings in outlook and behavior. A spate of difficult pastoral interventions, late-night crisis calls, demanding speaking engagements, and study assignments had left her lethargic and depleted in energy. When she finished describing her weariness I gave her a clean sheet of paper, asked her to draw two columns with the headings "Output" and "Input," and suggested that she list under each heading the various activities of her past two weeks. There was a complete imbalance. Twenty-five items featured in the first column and only two in the second. Inviting her to reflect upon this variance I asked her how she felt and what she was thinking. She sat quietly for a few minutes before answering, "Well, I feel tired when I compare the two lists. Obviously I don't replenish the energy I give out to others. I realize that I cannot keep giving out without taking time to resource myself. I must develop more balance in my life and find more sources of input. Perhaps God is even speaking to me in my tiredness and weariness about taking better care of myself."

My young friend's reply illustrates the value of practicing reflection. When we carve out the time in our busy schedules to reflect upon what's happening in our inner and outer worlds, those insights necessary for our ongoing growth become much clearer. In reflection we can look more closely at our daily activities. We observe our current approach to our activities and try to envision how we might carry them out more effectively. Most important of all, a reflective person can more easily discern the Divine Whisper within the emotions, circumstances, and events of daily life.

Examples from both Testaments supply supportive evidence for the value and practice of reflection. On the pages of the Old, Moses' solitary work of sheep-watching provided ample opportunity for him to think over his past experiences. Strikingly, against this backdrop God calls him through the burning-bush experience into the dual tasks of people liberation and nation building. (See Exodus 3:1-6.) Upon entering the world of the New Testament, Mary offers a model and mentor for the reflective life. Twice in Luke's Gospel the writer draws our attention to the way Mary remembered past experiences, pondered them in her heart, and mulled over their possible meanings. (See Luke 2:19, 51.) Without the commitment to a life of reflection, would these two personalities have been so wonderfully used by God as they were?

Reflection is the second essential ingredient of the pilgrimage experience. As the pilgrims reflect upon their encounters with suffering neighbors and become more aware of their inner responses, they uncover insights that can change their lives. Moreover, the practice of reflection fine-tunes their antennae to hear God speaking to them through the "human cries" around them, a kind of listening that often lays the basis for future actions of compassionate ministry and mission. I find that three particular activities facilitate the reflective lifestyle both on pilgrimage and in daily life:

- keeping a pilgrim journal,
- structuring a daily solitude time,
- sharing our experiences with one another.

Keeping a Pilgrim Journal

Each day of the Pilgrimage of Pain and Hope, participants are invited to record their reflections upon what their experiences. In their pilgrim journals, they record responses to both the outward and inward dimensions of the pilgrimage experience, which enables them to gain as much as they can from their privileged encounters with suffering people. Amid these daily reflections the pilgrims catch glimpses of their hidden hearts, discover insights necessary for their continuing conversion, and learn to discern the Divine Whisper. I suggest the following five questions as an aid to reflection:

- What did we do today?
- What encounter made the deepest impression on me?
- What are my thoughts and feelings about this encounter?
- What actions of hope and obedience did I see?
- What do I sense Christ saying through my day's experiences?

Three benefits flow out of this discipline of writing down reflections. First, keeping a pilgrim journal helps us track our significant experiences and encounters. Our memories are fallible. Many of us can hardly remember clearly what happened last week, let alone recall some of the thoughts and feelings that we had. In contrast, when we write out what takes place in our lives and record our inner responses, our reflections remain with us forever. We can return to a particular experience and remember its effect on us by reading the relevant page of our journal.

Second, keeping a pilgrim journal encourages us to persevere in the practice of reflection. Growing in self-knowledge and awareness evokes enormous resistance from within ourselves, especially when we start to discover aspects about ourselves that we would prefer not to know. In these moments the temptation to avoid the inner journey, to lose ourselves in compulsive busyness, and to focus on externals increases in intensity. Disciplining ourselves to find a quiet place to sit down with pen and paper and record our reflections on what is taking place in our lives helps us overcome this temptation and counter the resistant forces. Elizabeth O'Connor, a widely respected spiritual guide, offers this piece of wisdom:

> Among our primary tools for growth are *reflection, self-observation* and *self-questioning*. The journal is one of the most helpful vehicles we have for cultivating these great powers in ourselves. We all have these powers but we need structures that encourage us to use and practice them. Journal writing is enforced reflection. When we commit our observations to writing we are taking what is inside us and placing it outside us. We are holding a piece of our life in our hands where we can look at it, and meditate on it, and deepen our understanding of it.[1]

Third, keeping a pilgrim journal helps us to listen to God. Recall the earlier point made in chapter 2 about how the Divine Whisper usually takes the shape of a distinctive thought or feeling. If this be true, writing out affective responses to life helps us discern the still small voice. While not everything that surfaces into our consciousness comes from God, recording these movements of heart and mind on paper makes them concrete and allows us to sift through them more thoroughly. Using the five questions on page 60 we can then reflect upon our thoughts and feelings and ask the Holy Spirit to draw our attention to the Divine Whisper. Reflection practiced regularly along these lines leads us not only into greater self-understanding, but it also deepens our dialogue and communion with God.

I can personally vouch for the value of writing down reflections. About four or five times each week I sit down in a quiet place with Bible, journal, and pen. After spending some time meditating upon a passage from scripture, I jot down whatever comes to mind. Sometimes these thoughts and feelings relate directly to what I have just read; at other times they suggest practical tasks that need attention: people to see or things to do in my family relationships. They may emerge from past significant people-encounters, especially with those who suffer. Once I have finished writing, I then reread what is before me and ask the Holy Spirit to help me discern the Divine Whisper. As the following excerpt from a recent journal entry shows, these written meditations deepen my knowledge about myself, enable me to hear what God may be saying, and show me the way to go forward.

> Spent time yesterday with Gill in hospital. Presently she is suffering terribly from the horrendous effects of her chemotherapy treatment. I was deeply moved by our time together, and found myself struck by her re-

markable courage. When I mentioned this she answered quietly, "God gives this courage to all of us. We only need to use it." Her words echo within me as I sit here in the quiet. They remind me that there are buried assets in all of our lives, including my own. Lord Jesus, make me aware of those positive traits that lie dormant in my personality. Help me today to recognize in particular my capacity for courageous living and to develop it to your glory and for your sake.

STRUCTURING A DAILY SOLITUDE TIME

While we can practice reflection in the midst of activity and busyness, the truly reflective life requires time alone. Hence, on the Pilgrimage of Pain and Hope we program thirty minutes of solitude time into each day. During this time the pilgrims retreat to reflect on their encounters with suffering people, meditate on selected Bible passages, write in their journals, and pray. Without these solitary moments they probably would not do the reflective work so necessary for personal transformation and change. So closely are solitude and reflection connected that it is hard to imagine the one without the other.

In teasing out the threads that bind solitude with the reflective lifestyle, several closely related thoughts come to mind. To begin with, the experience of being alone creates the space in which we can gather ourselves together, relax, and become quieter within. It's nearly impossible to reflect deeply, either upon our lives or a Bible passage, when our bodies and minds are not at peace. By contrast, when we draw aside to some quiet place, we provide our souls with a proper environment in which to become still. Such stillness enables us to be in touch with our feelings and thoughts. We can better respond to whatever is taking place in our lives and become more sensitive to the Divine Whisper. No wonder we are advised, "Be still and know that I am God" (Ps. 46:10).

Another thought about this connection between solitude and reflection has to do with stopping in order to see more clearly. Some time ago we took a train trip as a family from Johannesburg to Cape Town. Early in the morning, as the train raced along, we looked out of the windows at the passing landscape. Traveling at such great speed made it difficult to register anything fully. Only when we stopped at the small stations could we fully take in the surrounding countryside. In a similar vein, our everyday lives become blurred when we stay constantly on the go. Solitude time, however, halts our rushing flow of experience so that we can gain clearer insight into what is churning around within and about us. In the well-known words of the sign at a railroad crossing, solitude allows us to STOP—LOOK—LISTEN.

Finally, solitude provides that quality of detachment required by all true reflection.[2] Only when we separate ourselves from our ordinary round of activities and pull ourselves loose from their clutches can we enter the reflective process. Moreover we become like Ping-Pong balls that bounce back and forth with every emotion and outward encounter, caught up in habitual ways of thinking and acting. In strong contrast, taking time out to be alone gives us the critical distance to step back from our experiences and think more objectively about them. After such solitude time and the reflection that accompanies it, we can reenter the world and respond more consciously and maturely to the challenges that confront us.

Detaching ourselves from our everyday involvements for brief time periods helps enormously when we battle with strong emotions. Again, the pilgrimage experience has been the laboratory for my learning in this regard. As the pilgrims encounter suffering and become increasingly aware of the human cries in their midst, difficult feelings often begin to surface in their lives. These can range from a paralyzing sense of powerlessness and inadequacy to deep distress, from fear and guilt to a cold indifference. Those who honestly write out their feelings and reflect upon them in solitude respond more constructively than those who avoid this inner work. Meaningful actions of ministry and mission, seemingly, are born out of a mature detachment penetrated by reflection and prayer.

In my everyday pilgrimage I find three kinds of solitude time necessary. Each day I enjoy taking "little solitudes," to use Catherine de Hueck Doherty's expressive phrase, in which to savor some time alone.[3] This may involve turning off the car radio as I commute or taking a five-minute break between counseling sessions or going for an evening stroll. During these quiet interludes I remind myself of God's companionship, meditate upon what's happening in my life, and listen for any gentle urgings that may be given about upcoming tasks. Also, before my working day begins I set aside some time—between twenty to forty minutes—for conversation with God built around the scriptures. And once a year I go away for a forty-eight-hour silent retreat where no phone or fax can interrupt. This yearly spiritual checkup allows for an in-depth look at my life, a reordering of priorities, and some goal setting for the future.

Sharing Our Experiences

The Pilgrimage of Pain and Hope is a journey shared with others. Pilgrims travel together in cars. We come together each day for at least one common meal. We meet for daily worship and discussion. We spend time playing as a group and, even when we separate to sleep over with our various hosts, we do so in pairs. During this time together we develop deep bonds of friendship and belonging that foster mutual encouragement, care, and celebration. When conflicts and disagreements arise, as they often do, we work through them in community. By the end of the pilgrimage the pilgrims have usually had a small but significant taste of genuine fellowship.

In all the ways described above, the pilgrimage experience embodies within its own communal life the corporate dimensions of the authentic Christ-following life. When we turn toward the crucified and risen Christ and open our hearts to receive him, he enters them with his arms around his sisters and brothers. We cannot say, "Lord Jesus, I want to be with you but not with your family." Genuine repentance and faith immerse the disciple in a common life. We follow Jesus bonded together with others who also have been called. Our growth in discipleship takes place within this family of belonging. To be in Christ and to progress toward maturity, requires community. Kenneth Leech holds together in creative tension the personal and corporate aspects of the life of faith when he writes the following:

Being a Christian, in the New Testament understanding, is thus not a purely personal, but a social reality. At the same time, within the body of Christ, there is an encounter with God, and a continuing and developing relationship with God, at the personal level.[4]

It follows that the practice of reflection, in order to be truly biblical, needs also to be done with others. For this reason each Pilgrimage of Pain and Hope has a time reserved for the sharing of personal experiences. Usually this life-sharing forms part of the liturgy for our daily worship. As we sit in a circle, each pilgrim is invited to share whatever he or she would like arising from their personal reflections in the solitude. On the first day of the pilgrimage the guidelines for this sharing process are discussed, clarified. and agreed upon. These helpful guidelines can be adapted for any group experience within the church:

- Everything shared within the group is strictly confidential.
- While every person is invited to share, no one is compelled to do so.
- When sharing, focus upon one's personal thoughts and feelings.
- When listening, do not interrupt or try to "fix" the person speaking.
- A brief silence follows each person's speaking for reflection on what has been said.
- Attendance is essential to our life together as a community.
- The facilitator may step in if the process goes astray or comment when everyone has finished sharing.

Many pilgrims find this group experience beneficial. In the process of articulating their personal thoughts and feelings and listening to those of others, they discover that their reflections expand and deepen. As they take turns to share, new insights emerge that open their eyes to what they had not seen before. Also, the activity of listening attentively to how another person perceives a certain reality or experience broadens their individual way of seeing. Like all of us with our own biases and prejudices, the pilgrims fall prey to the dangers of tunnel vision and so need to give careful attention to others' perceptions. Since God often shows one part of the picture to one person and another part to another person, this kind of mutual sharing goes a long way toward discerning what God may be saying through the various pilgrimage encounters.

I hope this chapter has encouraged you to develop a more reflective lifestyle. If it has, you may want to experiment with the following exercise. For a period of one week, commit yourself to a daily solitude time in which you can unplug yourself from your usual activities. In this quiet place yield yourself to God and ask for the gifts of divine wisdom and discernment. Record in a notebook your activities during the preceding twenty-four hours. Make notes of the people you encountered, the things you learned, your feelings, and the impressions you sense God wanted you to have. Remind yourself that God often speaks through our feelings and thoughts. Therefore, when you complete your daily journal entry, reread what you have written and ask the Holy Spirit to deepen your sensitivity to the Divine Whisper. At week's end evaluate your attempts at reflection and see whether they have made you more aware of God's presence in your everyday life. If they have, you may decide to practice reflection in this way on a regular basis. Whatever your decision, keep close to your heart Paulo Friere's admonition that unless we become reflective people we will never be among those "who will carry out radical transformations."[5]

INVITATION TO PILGRIMAGE

1. "We do not learn from experience; we learn from reflection upon experience." How do you respond to this statement?
2. How do you respond to the challenge of keeping a pilgrim journal?
3. What place does solitude have in your present way of life?
4. In what ways do you share your spiritual journey with others?
5. If you experimented with the suggested exercise over the past week, share your experience with the group.

Chapter 5

Becoming Compassionate Christ-Followers

❧

COMPASSION LIES at the heart of the authentic Christ-following life. Any spiritual experience—whether it be one of solitude and silence, prayer and fasting, or worship and celebration—that does not result in a deeper concern for our suffering neighbor can hardly be called Christian. The critical test of our relationship with the Holy One always involves the quality of our love for those around us. If our communion with God isolates us from the painful realities of our world, inoculates us against feeling the pain of our neighbors, and leads us into an excessive preoccupation with our own well-being, it must be considered suspect. If, on the other hand, it finds expression in greater compassion and a willingness to show care, then it passes the test for genuineness.

This authenticity test surfaces when we ponder the words and deeds of Jesus. Consider the parable of the Good Samaritan in this regard. A traveler on his way from Jerusalem to Jericho is mugged and left to die at the side of the road. Soon afterward a priest comes by and then a Levite, both of whom pass by without response. Finally a Samaritan stops, bandages the injured man's wounds, helps him onto his donkey, and takes him to a nearby inn where he continues to take care of him. Jesus ends the parable with a straightforward challenge to the listening lawyer, "Go and do likewise." The central message of this parable is hard to miss. Participation in the kingdom requires that we share with others the same kind of compassion that we have received from God and that we be humble enough to receive care from unlikely neighbors.

Jesus' deeds also press home this message. Compassionate caring characterizes his interactions with people, particularly his ministry to those in distress. The Gospels tell us that he touches the leper, responds to the hungry, opens the eyes of the blind and looks out upon the crowd who are like sheep without a shepherd with compassion. (See Mark 1:41; 8:2; Matthew 20:34; 9:36.) Scholars point out that the phrase used in these Gospel passages, "to be moved with compassion," is used exclusively with reference to Jesus or his Father. The relevant Greek verb, *splangchnizomai*, reveals the incredible depths of this compassionate response in the divine heart. In his reflections upon the noun from which this verb derives, Henri Nouwen comments,

> The *splangchna* are the entrails of the body, or as we might say today, the guts. They are the place where our most intimate and intense emotions are located. They are the centre from which both passionate love and passionate hate grow. When the gospels speak about Jesus' compassion as his being moved in the entrails they are expressing something very deep and mysterious. . . . When Jesus was moved to compassion, the source of all life trembled, the ground of all love burst open, and the abyss of God's immense, inexhaustible, and unfathomable tenderness revealed itself.[1]

Jesus' teaching and example demonstrates his "walking, talking compassion."[2] It follows that the life of discipleship involves becoming more compassionate. Such transformation comes about through the activity of the Holy Spirit working in us. We cannot, by our own efforts alone, change our hearts of stone into hearts of flesh. Nor can we study for a post-graduate degree in compassion! Compassion is a divine gift, made visible in those lives generously responsive to God and neighbor. The first two ingredients of the pilgrimage experience—*encounter* and *reflection*—merely ready us for the breakthrough of love. Using excerpts from the testimonies of the pilgrims, together with some reflections upon Jesus' word and deeds, I will describe what this compassion might look like when the third ingredient of *transformation* takes place.

AWARENESS

> Central to my experience of the Pilgrimage of Pain and Hope was that of deepened awareness. I became aware, for the first time in my life, of the tremendous pain experienced by the majority of our society—a pain so well camouflaged by the ruling government and manipulated media at the time. Encountering the pain and people involved firsthand—even though it was limited by time—brought home the reality far more deeply than watching a documentary on television. When leaving the places we visited, I knew I would never be the same again. To this day, even though much of the political horror has changed in South Africa, the Pilgrimage of Pain and Hope still remains embedded in my heart. The reality of people continuing to suffer daily due to poverty, crime, violence,

sickness, injustice, etc. still challenges me to question its nature and to contribute in some small way towards its solution. Within my own vocation as a pastor, I see my calling as raising awareness, helping people to open their eyes to see the suffering around them, to see the presence of the risen Christ in those who suffer and to work in partnership with God in bringing wholeness and healing.

—A pilgrim

Compassion, as this testimony suggests, flows from our becoming more aware of the human needs around us. Real awareness far exceeds the capacity of either information or rational analysis to effect lasting inner change. Before their participation in pilgrimage experience, many pilgrims already possess certain statistics about the issues of poverty, homelessness, drug abuse, and violence within the South African context. This knowledge, however, seldom engenders compassion. On the other hand, when these same pilgrims spend time with suffering people in these situations, share together a slice of life, and reflect upon these encounters, a fresh awareness of these painful realities is generated. More often than not, it is the kind of awareness that responds and finds expression in a deeply felt compassion and caring.

Jesus' responses to those around him demonstrate further this connection between compassion and awareness. Study his relationships with people, and you meet a man who comes across as being supremely aware and responsive. Consider briefly the following examples: he brings out into the open the critical thoughts of an antagonist, speaks exactly the right words to a paralyzed man, notices a desperate seeker of salvation hidden in a tree, and hears the cry of a blind beggar above the din of a noisy crowd. (See Luke 7:40-43; Mark 6:5; Luke 19:1-5; 18:35-40.) These incidents and others like them reveal Jesus' profound sensitivity to all who crossed his path. Perhaps the one Gospel sentence that best communicates his awareness is this: Jesus "needed no one to testify about anyone; for he himself knew what was in everyone" (John 2:25).

The Spirit's touch on our lives makes us more aware. As the Spirit filled Jesus and made him the most responsive and sensitive human being that ever lived, so the Spirit generates in us a similar current of awareness, gradually changing our hearts into the likeness of the compassionate Christ. On the pilgrimage experience I witness this Pentecostal work in the lives of many pilgrims. Hearts that open toward suffering neighbor in an attitude of receptivity, throb with new awareness. Their caring responses underline the truth of John Taylor's powerful assertion, "I would say that God the Spirit is the unceasing animator and communicator, the inexhaustible source of insight, awareness, recognition and response.[3]

Another vital dimension of this compassionate awareness initiated by the Spirit of God, when understood within the Christian tradition, is the recognition of Christ in the last, the least, and the lost. Recall that sentence spoken by Jesus in his parable on the Last Judgment, "Truly I tell you, just as you did it to one of the least of these who are members of my family, *you did it to me*" (Matt. 25:40, my italics). When the Holy Spirit breathes this sacramental awareness into our lives, it releases life-giving responses of compassionate caring. We realize that our care for those who suffer reveals the extent of our love for God and "that Christ in his poor is neither a case nor a cause, but a mystery before whom we bow even while we serve."[4] The more we enter this great mystery, the more we glimpse Christ reflected in the faces of those who suffer.

Mother Teresa's ministry on the streets of Calcutta witnessed powerfully to the compassionate consequences of recognizing Christ in the least of his family. Having taken that Gospel sentence from the parable of the Last Judgment to heart, she went about serving the poor and destitute as if she was serving Christ. When Malcolm Muggeridge, in a television documentary, questioned the motivation for Mother Teresa's actions, the humble Christ-follower distinguished her vocation from that of a social worker. When ministering to those who suffer, she and her team of nuns "do it to a Person." She truly believed that in caring for the poorest of the poor, she was alleviating the ongoing pain of Christ in our world.

Consider this experiment, which may help you open more deeply to this Spirit-generated current of awareness and recognition between yourself and your suffering neighbor. Next time you find yourself in the midst of a crowd, ask God to deepen your awareness of those around you who may be carrying heavy burdens. Usually I remind myself that every human being sits next to a pool of tears. Allow the presence of other people in all their inexhaustible mystery, burden, and need to impinge upon your awareness. Recognize the people near you as living sacraments of the Divine Presence, each of them potential Christ-bearers to our world. Intercede for those who seem particularly troubled and downhearted and lift them inwardly into the healing light and love of God. Later in the day reflect upon your experiment in awareness and record your responses in your pilgrim journal.

EMPATHY

> It was on the Pilgrimage of Pain and Hope that I was drawn out of my own little world into the bigger world of those in pain. At first I felt totally overwhelmed. After all what could I really do that would make a difference? But as the Pilgrimage progressed I slowly began to realize the importance of simply getting alongside suffering people and trying to understand life from their point of view. Even today when I meet someone in distress and pain, and there is little that I can do, I remind myself that I can try to be with him or her in what they are going through. This learning has made a great difference to the way I relate to others. When I am with people in pain I always try to look past outward appearances and attempt to put myself in their place.
>
> —A pilgrim

A second aspect of compassion, closely linked to new awareness, is empathy. The above quote from one pilgrim's testimony provides helpful clues into the rich meanings of this word. Empathy involves getting alongside others, being with them in whatever they are going through, and putting ourselves in their place. At its simplest level, this usually means sitting down with a person, taking time to listen, and trying our best to get his or her story right. More deeply however, empathy leads us into a close sharing of another's pain. We learn what it's like, in a small but significant way, to walk in our neighbor's shoes. This shared experience of suffering comprises the heart of true compassion. Again Nouwen expresses it well,

> Compassion asks us to go where it hurts, to enter into places of pain, to share in brokenness, fear, confusion

and anguish. Compassion challenges us to cry out with those in misery, to mourn with those who are lonely, to weep with those in tears. Compassion requires us to be weak with the weak, vulnerable with the vulnerable, and powerless with the powerless. Compassion means full immersion in the condition of being human.[5]

The shortest sentence in the Bible puts flesh on these words about empathy. In John 11 we read the dramatic events surrounding Lazarus's death and eventual rising to new life. Tucked away among the details of this story are the two words, "Jesus wept" (v. 35). Meditating upon this incident I am struck by the fact that Jesus weeps immediately after witnessing Mary's tears. This little detail suggests that Jesus cried not so much for Lazarus (surely he knew that he would soon be raising him from the dead), but rather that the grief of those around him had deeply moved his own heart. Jesus' tears in this scene show how completely God identifies with us in our suffering.

Part of me resists this challenge of identifying with suffering neighbor. Jesus' compassion sometimes scares me. Perhaps it scares you too. This could be why God's dealings with us include the rekindling of our longing to become more compassionate. We can acquire skills that promote the growth of empathy, like learning to listen in an active way, but in the final resort our hearts must be touched. And the good news that we have discovered from the pilgrimage experience is that, as we give ourselves to a real encounter with our suffering neighbor, the Spirit-breathed gift of compassion slowly takes shape in our hearts. Our responses to suffering change. Rather than wanting to avoid it at all costs, pilgrims experience an ever-deepening desire to get alongside those who suffer, listen to their stories, and be with them in their pain.

From the perspective of those in pain, the value of this kind of empathy cannot be overemphasized. My mind goes back to the frightening violence that preceded the first democratic elections in South Africa. During that time I found it deeply moving to witness on TV the presence of our church leaders with those who had suffered the loss of loved ones in the strife. Amid so much pain and anguish these leaders could do little. But they were *there*, offering their presence, getting alongside the grieving, listening to their words, sharing their pain, and praying with them. One mourner said in an interview, "It means everything to know that my bishop is with me at this terrible time."

ACTION

> The Pilgrimage of Pain and Hope has challenged me to become practically involved in the mission of Christ. I do not want to be a passive spectator any longer. The pilgrimage experience has taught me that the church is most effective when it is seen to be meeting the real needs of people. I want to be an active part of a Church that is relevant to the world outside its walls. I was also challenged to pursue my medical career in a way that will benefit most those on the underside of our society. I realized that it is not enough to be shocked or indignant at the life circumstances of people who suffer. If I am to follow the gospel way seriously I must be prepared to give my life in practical service as Christ gave his life for us.
>
> —A pilgrim

Compassion tries to respond practically in a situation of human suffering. Fifteen years after writing the above reflections upon his pilgrimage experience, this pilgrim continues to pour out his life in sacrificial service. With his wife and three children, he lives out his vocation as a doctor within a marginalized and disadvantaged community near Pretoria. He trains primary health-care workers, initiates self-employment opportunities for the unemployed, raises AIDS awareness among the school children, and generally uses his medical skills to make a creative difference in the lives of those around him. His example, hidden from the glare of the public spotlight, reminds me that compassion and practical action go together.

As usual Jesus leads the way in this regard. Compassion for him goes way beyond fleeting feelings of sympathy and pity; it expresses itself in practical actions aimed at relieving the pain and alienation of those who suffer. Gospel examples range from Jesus hugging a child, touching a leper, visiting the housebound, feeding the hungry, befriending the outcast to miracles of his healing the sick and raising the dead. (See Matthew 18:2; Mark 1:41; 1:30; Matthew 15:32; Luke 19:6; Matthew 11:4-5.) Passages like these show that compassion in the way of Jesus labors with the suffering for the sake of their greater well-being and wholeness. Learning to care as Jesus would, if he were in our place, means doing likewise. Controversial theologian Matthew Fox gets it right when he states,

> Biblical compassion resists the sentimentalizing of compassion. In Biblical spirituality the works of mercy

are *works* and the word for compassion in the Bible is more often employed as a verb than as a noun or an adjective. Compassion is about doing and relieving the pain of others, not merely emoting about it.[6]

Encountering those who do works of mercy encourages us to act similarly. Hence each Pilgrimage of Pain and Hope plans opportunities for its participants to meet with Christ-followers actively involved in compassionate ministry. On a recent pilgrimage experience we spent time with a church worker who ministers among the homeless, works alongside volunteers serving in a soup kitchen, speaks with a group of young people engaged in a year-long community service program, listens to hospice workers describe their experiences with the dying, and reflects with a missionary couple upon their church-planting efforts in an extremely disadvantaged community. These encounters with "signs of hope" impact the pilgrims greatly. They learn that ordinary people can be wonderfully used by God to bring healing and wholeness, if they willingly act on behalf of those who suffer.

As followers of Christ, we are not left in the dark to wonder about the precise nature of these compassionate actions. Besides the example of his own life, Jesus also speaks about six ways that authentic faith manifests itself. According to his parable on the Last Judgment, they are as follows: feeding the hungry, quenching thirst, welcoming strangers, clothing the naked, visiting the sick and those in prison. (See Matthew 25:35-36.) Certainly this list was not meant to be exhaustive. These works of mercy have a common denominator: all exhibit practical expressions of loving concern. We may add any action that leaves another person feeling more valued and loved. What matters is appropriate action in our care for others.

In seeking to express my compassion in a more concrete manner, I review regularly my responses to those who suffer. Little growth in compassion occurs until we face honestly how little care we usually manifest. Once we realize the poverty of our loving, we can ask God to help us do better. New beginnings take place when we recognize that our acts of love are few and then resolve to find practical ways to express the compassion we feel in our hearts. Questions like these below keep me sensitive to the gospel challenge of living a compassionate life. You may find it useful to pause and to consider them yourself.

- When did I last minister to the hungry, the thirsty, the homeless?

- How often have I gone out of my way to welcome strangers, especially those who are rather boring or unattractive?

- When was the last time I visited a sick person or someone who was bereaved or one of the many depressed and despairing in my midst?

- When have I reached out in person to those in prison or to someone who has recently been released?

- How do I show my care and concern on a daily basis to those around me, especially the suffering, broken, and hurt?

In drawing attention to the active ingredient of compassion, I introduce one cautionary note. Our best intentions on behalf of those who suffer go wrong when not attuned to their real needs. Too often in our sincere desires to be compassionate Christ-followers we engage in actions with no awareness of their effect upon those being "helped." They may find our attentions intrusive or cloying, patronizing, pretentious, or even false. Our caring may also undermine the dignity and initiative of those who suffer to take action themselves to remedy their situation. Sometimes, as Sister Margaret Magdalen wisely comments, our "*in*activity may well be the greatest mercy we could show."[7]

Compassion does not denote an extra commandment for the really serious disciple; it describes the essence of the true Christ-following life. We cannot call spirituality that does not make us more caring a gospel-spirituality. In light of Jesus' example and words, embarking along the compassionate way involves three primary tasks: becoming aware of those who suffer; being with them in their pain; and, where appropriate, acting together with them for the sake of their greater wholeness. Without the help and resources that come from the Spirit of God, we will not progress far along this road. Let us, therefore, pray that our hearts of stone become hearts of flesh.

Invitation to Pilgrimage

1. Describe *one* compassionate Christ-follower who has influenced your life.
2. Share your experience of the "awareness exercise" suggested on page 76.

3. How do you resist the challenge to become a compassionate Christ-follower?

4. What did you learn from your responses to the questions on page 82?

5. What *one* practical step can you take during the next few days that will express your intention to grow in compassion?

Chapter 6

Preventing Compassion Fatigue

M Y OWN WORDS surprised me. It was my Monday off, and I was sitting with someone I trusted a great deal. For over eighteen months we had met together on a regular basis for me to talk about how my life was going. On this particular afternoon, as we sat opposite each other, a heavy weariness hung over me. The prospect of going to work the next day and facing my pastoral responsibilities filled me with dread. Inside I felt drained, dried up, and despairing. When I expressed my thoughts and feelings, it seemed that I contradicted my deepest conviction about the Christ-following life. Struggling to keep my emotions under control, I said quietly, "I really don't want to care for people anymore."

My admission should not have surprised me. For some years a number of internal "indicator lights" had flashed on and off, cautioning me that I was on the edge of that condition known as compassion fatigue. Instead of paying attention to these inner warnings and revising the way I lived out my discipleship, I foolishly assumed that I could keep giving out without building into my life the necessary safeguards for my own well-being. Nor did

I realize then, as I do now, that overcaring could be unhealthy. I needed to discover a better balance between the two extremes of self-centeredness on the one hand and needless self-sacrifice on the other. Looking back, I can see that three specific indicator lights warned me about the deteriorating condition of my soul.

The first indicator light was that of the *increasing exhaustion* itself. In hindsight I realize that I allowed myself to become enmeshed in a downward spiral of caring activity. The dynamics of this vicious cycle were dangerously deceptive: when weary from being with those in need, I repeatedly sought to work through my tiredness by driving myself even harder. More often than not these extra caring efforts brought rewards of approval and appreciation which, by giving my flagging spirit a temporary high, camouflaged temporarily my worn-out condition. Thus I deceived myself into believing that I could keep on keeping on without replacing the energy used up in serving others.

Another indicator light was my *resentment toward the constant demands* made by those in need. Few other inner responses disturb Christ-followers more than this one, which often leaves them feeling guilty, ashamed, and unworthy. In my case, I hid my resentment behind a smiling face, judged myself harshly for these feelings, and drove myself even harder to show greater compassion. I became a "happy servant" on the outside, a "suffering martyr" on the inside. More recently I have recognized that these resentments do not always indicate selfishness; they sometimes express the legitimate longing of our souls for nurture. Acknowledging these soul needs and caring for them in appropriate ways frees us for deeper self-giving.

A third indicator light was the *lack of lightness and laugh-*

ter in my life. Seeking to live the compassionate life became a grim and heavy-hearted enterprise. Seldom did I enjoy moments of glad celebration, spontaneous joy, and carefree fun. I felt that enjoying myself betrayed the pain and anguish of those suffering around me. Unlike the joyful Nazarene in whose footsteps I sought to follow who was accused of being a wine-bibber and a glutton, I rarely accepted invitations to enjoy a good party. Not only did I view life through somber and dark spectacles, but even my picture of God assumed a rather gloomy countenance. My life had lost that balance between the celebrative and serious sides so necessary for personal wholeness and generous loving.

Can you identify with any of these warning signs? It's far better to recognize them early and take the necessary preventive action, than to arrive in the desperate place where I found myself. Since acknowledging the extent of my own weariness on that Monday afternoon, I have begun to forge a more balanced way of life. With the help of trusted soul friends, insights from scripture, and my closest family, I am engaging three behaviors that help me care in a healthier way:

1. becoming a compassionate neighbor to myself;
2. curbing tendencies toward compulsive caring;
3. developing a more celebrative lifestyle.

I outline them here with the hope that you find them meaningful in your own experience.

BECOMING A COMPASSIONATE NEIGHBOR TO MYSELF

Christ-followers who take seriously the gospel's challenge to compassion often neglect to care for themselves.

Whatever the reasons for this neglect (ranging from fear of doing anything that looks selfish, always wanting to please others, and needing to be needed to a sincere desire to put others first) inadequately caring for ourselves sets us up as prime candidates for compassion fatigue. We can care overmuch. Accepting the fact that we can care for others only when we care for ourselves guards us against the dangers of overcaring. Morton Kelsey underlines this insight when he writes, "Learning to be good Samaritans to ourselves is essential to becoming good Samaritans to others."[1]

Over time I have come to appreciate the wisdom of Kelsey's insight. When we do not show compassion toward ourselves, our compassion for others becomes poisoned with harmful toxins. However, once we learn to love ourselves as God does, we become freer to pour out our lives in sacrificial self-giving and to do so without resentment and heaviness of spirit. Having a proper love for ourselves, we can then forget ourselves, reach out to others, and respond to their needs. Self-love and other-love are bound together. Perhaps for this reason Jesus reaffirmed the centuries-old levitical command given to the Hebrew people as binding upon his followers: "You shall love your neighbor as yourself" (Matt. 22:39).

How do we become compassionate neighbors to ourselves? Here is a menu of possibilities worth exploring:

Take care of your body.
In caring for others we use up a great deal of physical and mental energy. If we do not replenish these limited resources, we run the risk of compassion fatigue. We cannot fulfill our God-given callings to be compassionate

human beings in bodies that are constantly neglected and overextended. How we feed, exercise, relax, listen to, and nourish our bodies are matters relevant to faithful discipleship. As Francis of Assisi lay dying, someone asked if he would have changed anything in his ministry. Significantly he responded, "I would have been more kind to my body."

I read some well-documented research regarding the healthy care of the body. Involving careful investigations into the lives of nearly seven thousand adults, the study recommends seven basic guidelines for good health. For a quick assessment of your care for your body, reflect upon your responses to the following suggestions: do not smoke, drink alcohol only in moderation, maintain appropriate weight, eat breakfast, don't eat between meals, exercise regularly (brisk walking is especially recommended), and get seven to eight hours sleep daily.[2]

Do what you enjoy.

Most people have a favorite spare-time activity. Whether it be working in the garden, walking in the countryside, playing sport, listening to music, reading for fun, developing a personal hobby, going to the movies, or simply enjoying a leisurely bath, these activities possess wonderful resourcing potential. When we omit activities like these from our lives—as those who care are prone to do—we end up living resentful, joyless, and frazzled lives. On the other hand, taking time to enjoy them renews energy levels, recharges inner batteries, and fills our empty tanks. If we want to give ourselves in compassionate caring, few aspects are more important than finding out what we enjoy doing—and doing it.

You can begin right now. Take a few moments to jot down all the activities that you enjoy. These activities don't need to be specifically religious. Select one that you can pursue in the next few days. Make sure you identify what *you*, and only *you*, would enjoy doing. This is a time for you to be yourself, to do what you want to do, without worrying about pleasing others. Next, budget some time for this pleasurable activity. After you have done it, write out your feelings and thoughts about the exercise. Notice especially its effects upon your capacity to give yourself away in deeper loving and caring for others. Above all, discern the goodness of God in the good you did for yourself, and give thanks for it.[3]

Process your own pain.

Each of us sits next to a pool of tears.[4] Some pools are deeper than others, but each of us has a pool of his or her own. These pools represent our grief about the experiences that have crushed our spirits, scarred our souls, and crippled our relationships. Trying to bring consolation and comfort to others in their pain without giving attention to these painful memories renders us vulnerable to compassion fatigue. However, finding a human wailing wall where we turn our pain into speech renews our capacities to live and love more deeply. Besides experiencing the loving presence of God in the care and counsel of those who listen to us, we also find out that processing our own pain helps us reach into the hearts of others who are in pain.

Permit me a brief word of testimony in this regard. Over the years numerous people have affirmed in my life the gift of listening. I spend large chunks of my daily time offering a listening presence to people in pain. The flipside of this listening gift was, however, that I seldom spoke about my own pain. Bottled-up feelings and emotions raged in my heart, longing for release. Some years ago I decided to find a safe place where I could share my heart. In the presence of a patient and skilled listener I found the courage to express my inner anguish—a liberating, healing, and humbling experience. This journey toward my own healing has not ended, but I know that without it I would be in no position to care for others.

CURBING TENDENCIES TOWARD COMPULSIVE CARING

Emphasizing compassion as the central value of the Christ-following life brings with it one great danger. It can encourage us to become compulsive carers. In his reflections upon this possibility, Gerald May writes about "addictive helpfulness" and invites his readers to identify their own automatic responses of showing compassion. He points out that we care compulsively when we ignore the tiny gap between feeling a person's pain and doing something for or to the suffering person. Consequently, when brought face-to-face with someone in need, we rush into the helpful role without first pausing to discern how best to express our compassion. May describes how these addictions of helpfulness are triggered when we are faced with human need,

> In a very computerlike way, our internal programs of what-to-do-in-a-situation-like-this are accessed and run. In a very uncomputerlike way, we don't even take the time to see which program is called for. There is no time. We must be about the business of being helpful.[5]

I witnessed an example of addictive helpfulness on a recent silent retreat. Early in the morning I came across a retreatant, who I knew was going through a difficult time, sobbing before the crucifix in the chapel. Knowing that she could freely ask for companionship and prayer from me if she wanted that, I left her alone. About an hour later I noticed another retreatant, arm around the distressed person, obviously seeking to bring comfort.

After the retreat I asked the retreatant who had been crying how she had found the silence. Her reply underlined how well-intentioned attempts at caring go badly astray when not attuned with what the one being "helped" really needs or wants. She replied, "Yesterday morning an old painful memory from childhood surfaced. I found myself grieving the loss in a way not experienced before. As I cried before the figure of the crucified Jesus I felt held in the loving presence of God. Unfortunately [here she named her "helper"] intruded into my silence. She insisted on sitting with me when all I needed was space. Her words and prayers really blocked the healing process. It took me almost the rest of the day to re-enter the deep place that I had touched before being interrupted."

Not only do our addictions of helpfulness fail the person for whom we care, they also open the door to compassion fatigue. When we disregard that vital space between feeling and response, we neglect the replenishing resources of the Spirit, exhaust ourselves in frantic do-gooding, and burn out. For this reason, seasoned associates of Jesus often mention the importance of attitudes like detachment, reticence, standing back, not doing too much, waiting, letting be, and letting go when they write about compassion. Such wisdom safeguards our caring from becoming intrusive, respects the space of our suffering neighbor, and energizes us for continued self-giving. Curbing tendencies towards compulsive caring benefits all parties involved in the helping relationship.

How do we begin to care less compulsively? First, we honor the gap between our feelings of care and compassion for someone and our desire to help immediately. When we feel another person's pain, rather than leaping into any set or predetermined active response, we acknowledge that we don't know exactly what this person needs. Our initial response must be simply our presence; we listen deeply and get alongside the suffering person. Inwardly, we direct a glance Godward and ask, "Lord, how would you have me respond here?" With this modest attitude we seek the whisperings of the Spirit, respect the mystery of our neighbor, and practice the art of compassionate nondoing. Reflecting upon what happens in this gap between feeling and response, Sister Margaret Magdalen writes helpfully:

> For in that space we have the chance to listen to what [others] really need, to listen to the Lord whose compassion it is that we invite to flow through us, and to discern how *he* would want us to incarnate and express it.[6]

Second, we care less compulsively when we set limits on our caring. Compulsive carers feel obliged to respond to every request that comes along. Often promising to do more than they can possibly deliver, they no set limits and find themselves living amid the debris of broken promises and disappointed expectations. If you recognize yourself in these words, consider again the realism of Jesus who did not respond to every need but rather singled out those he could help. Similarly, surrounded as we are by staggering human need, we cannot take all the world's pain upon our shoulders. Like Jesus, the best we can do is discern where we can express care and invest our energies there. In this way we guard ourselves against the dangers of addictive helpfulness, show respect for our own limitations, and discover how to share wisely the love we have received from God.

Third, we care less compulsively when we allow others to care for us. One of the hardest things for carers is to acknowledge their own neediness, to ask for help and receive the compassion of loved ones and friends. I once took part in a foot-washing ceremony during Holy Week. I found myself quite at home washing the feet of others. But when it came to having my feet washed I wanted to get up and leave the room. An insidious pride had disabled me in receiving from others. Maybe all who desire to become compassionate Christ-followers need to stick a new Beatitude on their fridges that reads, "Blessed are those who are able to receive care from others, for they are able truly to care for others."

Take a few moments to reflect on the way you care for others. Three straightforward yes / no questions may aid your reflections:

- Do you usually rush into an active helping role when faced with someone in need?

- Do you often experience weariness from taking on too many caring responsibilities?

- Do you normally struggle to share your needs with others?

Should you answer yes to any of the above, you may need to join me in curbing tendencies toward compulsive caring. Otherwise you may be heading for compassion fatigue without even knowing it.

Developing a Celebrative Lifestyle

Joy is the primary antidote given to us by God for the prevention of compassion fatigue. In our pursuit of compassionate discipleship, it constitutes our first line of defense against weariness, resentment, and despondency. Scripture teaches that the joy of the Lord is our strength. (See Nehemiah 8:10.) Joy keeps us going, renews our energy, and makes us strong. On the other hand, joylessness diminishes our capacity for self-giving and renders us vulnerable to those things that cause burnout. It's not surprising that the apostle Paul wants joy to become an essential ingredient in the lives of all Christ-followers. Writing to the young Christian churches he invites them repeatedly to rejoice, no matter what they are going through. (See Philippians 3:1; 4:4; 1 Thessalonians 5:16.)

In our ravaged world, where evil appears to be stronger than good, some may protest against this insistence upon joy. Indeed, we may have every reason not to be full of joy; but we can *choose* a life of joy and do those activities and attitudes that open our lives to it. The biblical writers' frequent command to be joyful implies that joy is both a gift and a duty. Joy does not happen automatically. In the breathtaking knowledge that the risen Christ has decisively overcome the powers of darkness and death and that nothing can ever separate us from God's loving presence, we have to choose joy. For some, especially if they have suffered greatly, this choice may well be the greatest challenge of their faith.

We open our lives to God's gift of joy by developing a celebrative lifestyle. In spite of the emphasis upon feast days and festivals in the Old Testament, and Jesus' first public miracle when he aided the wedding celebration by turning water into wine, celebration may rank as one of the most neglected and misunderstood disciplines of the spiritual life. Biblical writers assumed that times of feasting and festivity could build one's relationship with God just as much as regular times of solitude and prayer. Usually celebration involves coming together with God's people to eat and drink, sing and dance, pray and play and to tell stories of God's action and presence in our lives. Dallas Willard describes spiritual celebration in this way: "We engage in celebration when we enjoy ourselves, our life, our world *in conjunction with* our faith and confidence in God's greatness, beauty and goodness."[7]

My favorite description of celebration as a spiritual discipline occurs in the guidelines given in the fourteenth chapter of Deuteronomy. There the people of God are instructed to set apart a tithe of their yearly produce, transport it to Jerusalem, and enjoy a feast in the presence of the Lord. If the distance proved too far for the goods to be taken to the great city, the tithe was to be converted into money and spent on "whatever you wish—oxen, sheep, wine, strong drink, or whatever you desire. And you shall eat there in the presence of the LORD your God, you and your household rejoicing together" (v. 26). Moreover, persons were to invite outsiders in to share in the feast. Imagine the joy as God's people came together and renewed their faith in this down-to-earth and pleasurable way.

While it would be misguided to use this Old Testament passage as an excuse for drunkenness, it does invite us to find earthy ways of celebrating together. Recently a small group to which I belong decided to experiment with the spiritual discipline of celebration. Together we planned an evening that enabled us all, both adults and children, to celebrate our belonging in Christ. It was a joy-filled night.

Each family brought a plate of specially prepared eats, a beverage, and their favorite music. The evening began with an icebreaker during which all spoke about something good that had happened in their lives during the past week. We spent time worshiping together, clapping our hands, and making a joyful noise as we sang some of our favorite spiritual songs. Around the candlelit table, against the background of gentle music, we ate and drank, told stories, shared snippets of news and enjoyed one another's company. The evening ended as we held hands together and gave thanks for the goodness of God. Afterward I felt nourished in my faith and strengthened to take up the responsibilities of my everyday life with greater love.

I hope that this has whetted your appetite for a more celebrative lifestyle, which can begin in many small ways. Allow mealtimes to become daily celebrations where everyone joins in conversation and laughs together; turn family events such as birthdays and anniversaries into occasions of fun and thanksgiving; wear clothes that make you feel happy to be alive; delight in the colors and textures of the natural world around you; spend leisure time relaxing with friends and family—and, as you do these, relish these experiences, enjoy the generous goodness of God. If you belong to a small group or local congregation, initiate discussions about how you can celebrate together as members of God's family. Take advantage of the great festivals of our faith—Christmas, Easter, Ascension, and Pentecost—and build around them times of recollection and rejoicing. As you explore these possibilities, ponder the words of Jean Vanier,

> We must learn to celebrate. I say *learn* to celebrate, because celebration is not just a spontaneous event. We have to discover what celebration is. Our world doesn't know much about celebration. We know quite a bit about parties, where we are artificially stimulated with alcohol to have fun. We know what movies and distractions are. But do we know what celebration is? Do we know how to celebrate our togetherness, our being one body? Do we really know how to use all that is human and divine to celebrate together?[8]

Compassion fatigue may be God's way of getting our attention when our caring goes awry. This was true for me. Thankfully, today I am more aware of the shadow side of compassion and am slowly discovering how to care in a more life-giving way. As I become a compassionate neighbor to myself, curb my tendencies toward compulsive caring, and develop a celebrative lifestyle, I find that I have more to give to others. And so, in your reaching out to your suffering neighbor, do not neglect your own needs; beware of addictive helpfulness; and, above all, learn to celebrate.

Invitation to Pilgrimage

1. Can you describe a time of compassion fatigue from your own experience?

2. In what *one* way can you better care for yourself?

3. Identify *one* symptom of addictive helpfulness in your life.

4. Do you enjoy God? If so, how?

5. Discuss possibilities for a group celebration and select one that you can pursue together in the near future.

Chapter 7

Making the Pilgrimage
Part of Daily Life

AFTER EACH PILGRIMAGE the pilgrims share their experiences in a variety of church settings. These testimony opportunities allow them to articulate what has taken place in their lives, and their stories encourage others to consider going on pilgrimage. One young mother approached me after the pilgrims spoke at an evening service. Their testimonies had affected her deeply, awakening a strong desire to go on the next pilgrimage. But with a demanding job and two small children she had little hope that she could get away from home.

I still remember her question: "Is there any way I can go on pilgrimage right where I live?" It was a good question. We have noted how the gospel invitation breathes the adventure of pilgrimage into the hearts of all who respond. When Jesus says, "Follow me, " he calls each one of us to make our unique journey into the heart and life of God. The early Christ-followers understood this and so described themselves as people of the Way. (See Acts 9:2; 18:25; 19:9, 23; 22:4; 24:14, 22.) Imagine how this self-description nurtured the pilgrimage metaphor in their hearts and minds. No longer were they drifters, unsure of who they were or where they were going. Now they saw themselves as pilgrims on a journey, traveling together along the discipleship road. And this is how God wants us to see ourselves as we respond to the call of Christ. Alan Jones describes it well,

> The challenge of the gospel is, Will you allow your drifting to be consecrated into pilgrimage? Will you entertain the possibility that you matter, that you are here for a purpose, that you have a mission that no one else can fulfill?[1]

As Christ-followers we are called to reflect his compassionate heart. Compassion and communion with a loving God belong together. Around this basic conviction the Pilgrimage of Pain and Hope has been presented as a means of spiritual formation and growth. Exposing participants to their suffering neighbor in personal encounter, drawing their attention to hope-creating responses, and inviting reflection upon their experience fosters a climate for discipleship growth that honors the centrality of compassion. It would be sad if only those able to leave domestic responsibilities could participate. I have discovered at least three ways in which we can become pilgrims in our daily lives.

WAITING SILENTLY

We make the pilgrimage experience part of our daily lives by cultivating the practice of sitting still and waiting in expectant silence. Throughout this book my description of the Pilgrimage of Pain and Hope has been interspersed with references to solitude, silence, and reflection. Unless we honor this inward dimension of the pilgrimage experience, our growth into becoming compassionate Christ-followers degenerates into barren activism. Caring workaholics, while correcting what has been called a "false inwardness," seldom make faithful pilgrims. Frantic do-gooding dulls our responses to the Divine Whisper, depletes our spiritual resources, and often ends up in cynicism and despair. Aspiring pilgrims do well to heed the words of the psalmist, "Be still before the LORD, and wait patiently for him" (Ps. 37:7).

The Quakers demonstrate powerfully the relevance of this verse for all who care for others. Few groups have contributed as much to peacemaking, a culture of non-violence, relief of suffering, and the struggle for justice as they have. Yet they cannot be accused of promoting a barren activism. Underpinning their vibrant social witness lies a highly effective and careful ritual for the practice of silent, expectant waiting. I was told that in front of the Friends' meeting house in Cambridge a sign reads, "Don't just do something . . . SIT!" In a contemporary church environment that encourages us to overextend ourselves in much doing, this sounds like timely advice. As Kenneth Leech wisely observes,

> The hyperactive person, whether community worker or pastor, who has not given time for inner stillness will soon communicate to others nothing more than his or her inner tiredness and exhaustion of spirit—not a very kind thing to do to people who have enough problems of their own.[2]

The biblical word *rest* describes well this practice of sitting still in silent, expectant waiting. "Come to me, all you that are weary and are carrying heavy burdens," says Jesus, "and I will give you rest" (Matt. 11:28). In this inner resting place we release dependence upon words, lay aside busy thoughts, and put down constant doing. Instead, we let God be God and soak up that unconditional acceptance and merciful love. Persevering in this quiet way of prayer renews our spirits, refreshes our souls, and replenishes our energies. Fresh streams of life-giving compassion begin to flow outward from our depths. Connecting with the source of love in the still center of our beings empowers us to care more deeply for others.

A delightful story about Abba Antony, one of the Desert Fathers, presses home the importance of this resting in God. One day a hunter came across Abba Antony and his brothers relaxing in the forest. The hunter expressed his surprise that so pious a man as Antony could sit and do nothing. Abba Antony invited the hunter to put an arrow in his bow and shoot it, which he did. Then the hermit asked him to shoot another and another and another. The hunter protested that if he continued shooting without a rest, the bow would break. Antony answered, "So it is the same in the work of God. If we push ourselves beyond measure, we will break; it is right for us from time to time, to rest and relax our efforts."[3] When we sit still in silent, expectant waiting, we rest the bow and allow God to strengthen us for ongoing ministry.

Given the unique way that God deals with each of us and our vastly different personalities, there will be a rich diversity in the ways we enter our inner rest in God's presence. Some find it helpful to choose a simple word or phrase, expressive of their longing for God, that they keep in their awareness. Examples range from single words like

Abba, Jesus, Maranatha to the well-known Jesus Prayer, "Lord Jesus Christ, Son of God, have mercy on me, a sinner." Repeating our prayer word or phrase for twenty minutes or so and gently returning to it when our attention wanders leads us into a restful place where we can attach ourselves more deeply to God. Others prefer to gaze at a picture or a symbol—a lighted candle, a crucifix, a single flower, an ancient icon—while they focus their hearts and minds on God. Whatever method used, the challenge is to create a little pool of inner stillness in which to learn to "know that I am God" (Ps. 46:10).

LOVING SPECIAL NEIGHBORS

We make the pilgrimage experience part of our daily lives when we journey into deeper relationships with those closest to us. Our first priority in caring is always our special neighbors with whom we share our lives—our spouses, children, siblings, parents, and close friends. Few instances are more hypocritical than caring for distant neighbors at the expense of these family and friends. One sure sign that we need to stop and reexamine our priorities occurs when serving others ruins our intimate relationships. Dr. Carl Jung once made a brief but telling comment on this issue. A friend was talking to him about a certain man who was doing much good and what a saint he was; Jung with a twinkle in his eye, responded, "Oh, but I would want to meet his wife and children before I decided on his sainthood."

Turning intimate relationships into opportunities for pilgrimage does not happen automatically. The alarmingly high incidences of divorce, marital breakdown, and relationship pain make this clear. We struggle to love even those we have chosen. Furthermore, if reared in families characterized by constant tension, unresolved conflict, emotional coldness, and physical abuse, our ability to relate warmly may be hindered. The good news is that we can learn how to relate more intimately in our relationships. The pilgrimage experience, with its three ingredients of *Encounter—Reflection—Transformation* has much to teach us. When we spend time with loved ones and reflect upon these encounters, we open our relationships to transformation and change. Notice the relevance of each ingredient for our journey into deeper relationships.

First, the pilgrimage experience underlines the importance of spending time with our special neighbors. Real encounter seldom happens in a hurry. If we really care or want to care for someone close, then we need to spend unhurried time with that person alone. As I say to couples on their wedding day, "Love is spelled T-I-M-E." Recently I learned that Susannah Wesley, the mother of John and Charles, had twenty children and yet managed to spend an hour a week alone with each of them. Eleven of the children became religious, political, and literary figures in eighteenth-century England. Journeying into deeper relationships within our family and friendship circles requires this kind of time commitment. As Morton Kelsey points out, "Love cannot be expressed without making time for the person whom we would love."[4]

Second, the pilgrimage experience encourages reflection upon our responses in our relationships. Unless we stop and face honestly how we actually do relate, we will not grow in compassion. Spending time with our special neighbors and encountering their needs and shortcomings evokes deep emotional responses. Not only are our tendencies towards self-centeredness exposed, we also receive glimpses of our potential for sacrificial loving. Taking time to reflect upon how we behave sensitizes us to these Spirit-generated awarenesses, facilitates better loving choices for the future, and helps us move toward becoming the person God wants us to be. Indeed, we seldom journey into deeper relationships until we honestly consider how we do relate most of the time. Two questions may expedite this reflective process :

- How did I give and receive love today?
- How did I fail to give and receive love today?

Third, the pilgrimage experience invites us to risk relating to our special neighbor in transformed ways. Possibilities for personal growth and ongoing conversion abound in our close relationships, especially when we view them from a pilgrimage perspective. Through reflection upon our ways of relating, God may call us to show our natural feelings of warmth and affection or engage in some random acts of kindness or give our partner more space or stop our unhealthy withdrawal patterns or learn how to ask for what we need. As we respond to these divine invitations, God inevitably empowers us with gracious and constant companionship. In the final analysis, our growth in loving always comes as a gift and not as the result of our own efforts alone.

Recently I spent time counseling a young married couple. They asked for an appointment because they felt their marriage had become stagnant. "Our relationship stopped growing on our wedding day," explained the wife at our initial meeting, "and we've been stuck ever since."

Together we explored ways of seeing marriage as an opportunity to go on pilgrimage into a deeper intimacy and friendship. They made regular appointments for time together alone, reflected daily on the two questions suggested above, and began viewing their marriage as God's means for their personal growth toward wholeness. In our final interview the husband remarked, "It makes all the difference to see marriage, not as a destination, but as a journey." They had become pilgrims in daily life!

CONNECTING WITH SUFFERING

We make the pilgrimage experience part of our daily lives by connecting with suffering. We have repeatedly noted that Christ through his Spirit forms his compassionate heart in us. Transformation is the gift and work of God. Yet the moment we affirm this, we need not make the mistake of saying that we can do nothing. Indeed, only through a disciplined life can the transforming grace of God flow into our lives. Traditionally, when Christian writers mention spiritual disciplines, the lists have included the disciplines of solitude, prayer, Bible reading, fasting, fellowship, worship, and the like. In the light of the pilgrimage experience I want to emphasize one discipline seldom mentioned: planned encounter with those who suffer in our midst.

I encourage you to begin simply. Commit yourself to spend a certain portion of your week—perhaps an hour, an afternoon, or an evening—with someone who suffers. This person may be in prison, terminally ill, severely disadvantaged either physically or mentally, economically impoverished, or stuck in dark depression. As you plan to spend time with this person, remember the importance of cultivating a pilgrim attitude. (See chapter 3.) Rather than rushing in with help or advice, the emphasis of your time together is being present, listening, and becoming aware. Remind yourself that Christ promises to meet us in those who suffer. Do not underestimate what your simple presence may mean. After each visit, take time to reflect, write out your feelings and thoughts, and notice whether God is saying anything to you.

Like any other spiritual discipline, it's not always easy to stick with this commitment. Often we will find excuses to opt out or to do something more "productive" with our time. Nonetheless, as we persevere in this discipline in the faith that God will meet us, we change. We find ourselves becoming more responsive and aware, more sensitive to the pain around us. The Spirit of God is at work, opening our eyes, enlarging our hearts, and shaping us into the compassionate people God calls us to be. Through these planned exposures to people in pain, we may hear God's call into a specific avenue of ministry. We discover that we are here for a purpose and that we have a mission no one else can fulfill.

This happened for Hazel van Rensburg, a married mother with three sons who works as a freelance columnist. After attending a seminar where we explored this pilgrimage discipline of connecting with suffering, Hazel sought and received permission to visit women in her city's prison on a weekly basis. It was the beginning of a profound inner and outer spiritual journey. Not only did Hazel discover what it means to really care, she found herself ministered to in remarkable ways. In an article she wrote for a national magazine she described her experiences. Here are a few brief extracts.

"Spend at least an hour a week with someone who suffers." These were Reverend Trevor Hudson's closing words at a mission on the devotional life which I attended a few years ago. Words that for me would mark the beginning of a prison ministry which added a new dimension to my life as a Christian.

I remember clearly some of my expectations as I started out as a spiritual worker among the women prisoners in the city prison. I had aspirations of Bible study sessions which would revolutionize their lives. I visualized myself face to face with Jesus one day (trumpets sounding!) accompanied by a host of ex-prisoners who had met the Lord in prison.

Ironically, it was those very expectations which were to humble me: I wanted to do the work only the Holy Spirit could do, namely to change these women. I was to experience defeat and disappointment. I was to learn to persevere and to be patient. These women were running on empty. After six months my only achievement seemed to be that they now smiled at me when they saw me.

Of the many obstacles I would encounter was the uncomfortable feeling I had that the prisoners saw me as a kind of "hanging judge" armed with a Bible and not to be trusted. Before I could do anything else, I had to show them that I really cared about them, that I was on their side, and that they mattered. I was not to judge and I was not to pry. They had to trust me.

Three months later I was to experience the glorious wonder of being ministered to while ministering. I was dealt a devastating blow when my younger brother died unexpectedly. I experienced grief I had never known. Consequently I did not feel inclined to visit the prison the next day, but somehow found myself there at the usual time.

I always started off my session with a caring question to each woman individually: "What is in your heart today?" One young girl—barely eighteen—shared the same agony every time: "I just wish I could turn the clock back."

But on that Sunday it was *my* heart that was so burdened that I shared my sorrow with them instead: "I wasn't even able to say goodbye to him," I confessed, the lump in my throat so thick that my words were hardly audible. I was overwhelmed by their love and compassion. No one had wept with me until then. . . . These women, each with a criminal record, apparently the *least* in society and who had themselves experienced the harsh bite of pain and lonely nights of grief, were the people used by God that Sunday afternoon to help lead me out of the valley of the shadow.

FINALLY

Our world has become a global village, exposing us to an indescribable amount of human misery. We cannot take responsibility for it all. We cannot feed *all* the hungry, visit *all* the sick, care for *all* the bereaved, befriend *all* the depressed, and reach out to *all* the strangers. But we can, in silent, expectant waiting, discern where the Lord wants us to reach out in compassion and plan our time accordingly. If confined to home, we can always intercede or materially support ministry among the needy. We can also call someone who is hurting or send a card or answer a letter. In some specific way, each one of us can build the pilgrimage experience into our daily lives by connecting personally with suffering.

Our times cry out for a mass movement of compassion. This urgent need coincides with the goal of the Christ-following life, for unless our faith makes us compassionate it can hardly be called Christian. Following Jesus means moving out of our privatized, isolated, and self-enclosed worlds into a compassionate engagement with our suffering neighbor. As we open ourselves to the pilgrimage experience, either by going on a Pilgrimage of Pain and Hope or by building its key ingredients into our daily lives, we journey from self-centeredness to compassion. May you and I become everyday pilgrims whom God can use to bring healing to our broken world.

INVITATION TO PILGRIMAGE

1. Would you see yourself as a drifter or a pilgrim?
2. Tell about your personal experience with stillness and silence.
3. Share *one* struggle you encounter in loving your special neighbors.
4. Share *one* intention that you may have about connecting with suffering.
5. What are your plans to become a pilgrim in daily life?

Appendix

Planning a Pilgrimage
for a Local Congregation

As a result of reading this book you may want to plan a Pilgrimage of Pain and Hope in your own congregation. Here are ten "travel tips" that may help:

1. *Introduce the basic idea to the leadership of your local church.* Let chapter 1, "Introducing the Pilgrimage Experience," guide you in preparing your presentation. Make sure you communicate clearly the basic aims and underlying philosophy of the pilgrimage experience. (See "Essential Pilgrimage Ingredients" on page 19.) Express your willingness to take responsibility for the planning process.

2. *Sound the call for the formation of a pilgrimage planning team.* Should the leadership give permission for a Pilgrimage of Pain and Hope, ask the wider congregation if anyone would like to join you in further exploration and planning. Set a date to meet with those who respond. Suggest at your first meeting that, in order to plan a local pilgrimage experience, it may help to spend a few weeks going through this book together.

3. *Decide the length of your pilgrimage experience.* In determining how long your pilgrimage will be, take into account the age group and circumstances of those you want to attract. Possibilities range from a week-long pilgrimage experience for younger people to a weekend or one-day event for those with families.

4. *Choose the places you would like to go.* Possibilities include the following:
    *   counseling center
    *   awareness walk in an unfamiliar part of your town or city
    *   facility for those with mentally handicapping conditions
    *   healing center
    *   hospice
    *   inner-city congregation
    *   job-creation projects
    *   rehabilitation center for recovering addicts
    *   shelter for the homeless
    *   street ministries

    Add other possible venues from your knowledge of the local community. Plan one *exposure event* per day.

5. *Link up with "bridge-person/s" already present in the place/s you intend to visit.* This person might be a co-ordinator of a service organization, a community worker, a local pastor or priest, or a respected resident within a particular neighborhood. Make contact, introduce yourself, and outline the purpose of your intended visit. Make it clear that you are com-

ing to listen and learn. Discuss possibilities of conversation with those involved in active ministry, as well as with those who embody the "human cry" of the community.

6. *Draw up a detailed daily itinerary.* Ensure that you set time aside each day for encounter, reflection, worship, and fun. Here is one example taken from our last pilgrimage when we visited a rehabilitation center for recovering addicts.

9:00 AM Pilgrims meet together at the local church for thirty minutes of worship and prayer.

9:30 AM Arrive at Rehabilitation Centre and have tea with coordinator.

10:00 AM Coordinator shares the Center's vision and explains the extent of the need.

11:30 AM Pilgrims sit in on group session with some of the recovering addicts.

1:00 PM Lunch with staff and residents.

2:00 PM Pilgrims spend time individually with residents.

3:30 PM Pilgrims return to local church and spend time reflecting upon the day. (See "Keeping a Pilgrim Journal," page 60 and "Structuring a Daily Solitude Time," page 63.)

4:30 PM Group-sharing time. (See "Sharing Our Experiences," page 66.)

6:00 PM Light supper together at local shopping center before pilgrims meet their hosts again at the local church.

7. *Form the pilgrim group that will go on pilgrimage.* You can do this by inviting individuals personally and also by circulating information in the local church or fellowship. Spend time with each applicant going over the basic philosophy of the pilgrimage experience. Ten to fifteen pilgrims is an optimum number.

8. *Plan a "pilgrimage preparation day."* Using the contents of chapter 2, "Preparing for Pilgrimage," explore the three ingredients of a pilgrim posture: learning to be present, learning to listen, and learning to notice. It may help to do the exercises outlined in chapter 2, as well as answer the questions under "Invitation to Pilgrimage" at the end of the chapter.

9. *Examine the dynamics of reentry.* Near the end of the pilgrimage experience, ask the pilgrims to list their concerns as they prepare to reenter their home situations. Discuss these together and outline possibilities for ongoing spiritual direction and pastoral support. Explore together what it may mean to make pilgrimage part of daily life. (See chapter 7, "Making the Pilgrimage Part of Daily Life.") Ask the pilgrims to write *one* paragraph about their pilgrimage experience, beginning with the words, "On the Pilgrimage of Pain and Hope it has become clear to me that. . . . "

10. *Provide testimony opportunities.* After the pilgrimage experience, allow the pilgrims to tell their stories

among the wider congregation. Encourage the pilgrims to build their testimonies around the themes of awareness, empathy, and action. (See examples in chapter 5, "Becoming Compassionate Christ-Followers.") Besides encouraging others to consider going on a Pilgrimage of Pain and Hope, these testimonies help the pilgrims integrate their own experiences more deeply.

Notes

CHAPTER 1 INTRODUCING THE PILGRIMAGE EXPERIENCE

1. Trevor Hudson, *Christ-Following* (London: Hodder & Stoughton, 1996), 94.

CHAPTER 2 PREPARING FOR PILGRIMAGE

1. Eugene Peterson, *A Long Obedience in the Same Direction* (Downers Grove, Ill.: InterVarsity Press, 1980), 12.

2. Douglas Steere, *Together in Solitude* (New York, N.Y.: Crossroad Publishers, 1982), 176.

3. Catherine de Hueck Doherty, *Poustinia* (New York N.Y.: Ave Maria Press, 1975), 69.

4. Metropolitan Antony, *School for Prayer* (London: Day-break, 1970), 53.

5. Morton Kelsey, *Caring* (Mahwah, N.J.: Paulist Press, 1981), 72.

6. I describe this process of discernment at greater length in *Invitations to Abundant Life* (Cape Town: Struik, 1998), 46–48.

CHAPTER 3 ENCOUNTERING OUR SUFFERING
NEIGHBOR

1. Taken from Douglas Steere's *Gleanings* (Nashville, Tenn.: The Upper Room, 1986), 67.

2. John Claypool, *Opening Blind Eyes* (Nashville, Tenn.: Abingdon Press, 1983), 107.

3. I first came across this legend in Richard Foster's *Prayer* (London: Hodder & Stoughton, 1992), 266.

4. Jean Vanier, *From Brokenness to Community* (Mahwah, N.J.: Paulist Press, 1992), 19.

5. I learned this prayer exercise from author Morton Kelsey.

6. I also recount this story in my book *Christ-Following* (London: Hodder & Stoughton, 1996).

CHAPTER 4 REFLECTING UPON OUR EXPERIENCES

1. Elizabeth O'Connor, *Letters to Scattered Pilgrims* (New York, N. Y.: Harper and Row, 1979), 38.

2. I am indebted to Morton Kelsey for this insight. In his book *The Other Side of Silence* (London: SPCK, 1977) he distinguishes helpfully between a mature detachment that leads to a responsible living in the world and the kind that results in a pathological and distorted denial of life. (See pages 125–29).

3. Catherine De Hueck Doherty, *Poustinia* (New York, N.Y.: Ave Maria Press, 1975), 22.

4. Kenneth Leech, *True God* (London: Sheldon Press, 1985), 119.

5. Quoted by Elizabeth O'Connor in her book, *The New Community* (New York: Harper and Row, 1976), 109.

CHAPTER 5   BECOMING COMPASSIONATE CHRIST-FOLLOWERS

1. Henri Nouwen, *Compassion* (New York, N.Y.: Doubleday & Company, 1982), 16.
2. Sue Monk Kidd, *When the Heart Waits* (San Francisco: HarperCollins, 1990), 202.
3. John V. Taylor, *A Matter of Life and Death* (London: SCM Press, 1986), 10.
4. John V. Taylor, *The Go-Between God* (London: SCM Press, 1972), 242.
5. Henri Nouwen, op. cit., 4.
6. Matthew Fox, *A Spirituality Named Compassion* (Minneapolis, Minn.: Winston Press, 1979), 7.
7. Sister Margaret Magdalen, *Furnace of the Heart* (London: Darton, Longman & Todd Ltd., 1998), 94.

CHAPTER 6   PREVENTING COMPASSION FATIGUE

1. Morton Kelsey, *Set Your Hearts on the Greatest Gift* (New York: New City Press, 1996), 95.
2. I came across the "Seven Basic Rules of Good Health" in *The Joy of Feeling Good* by William Miller (Minneapolis, Minn.: Augsburg Publishing House).
3. I have adapted this exercise from Wanda Nash's book *Turning the Downside Up* (London: HarperCollins), 88.
4. It was in a conversation with Gordon Cosby that I first heard the phrase "pool of tears."

5. Gerald May, *The Awakened Heart* (New York, N.Y.: HarperCollins, 1991), 237.

6. Sister Margaret Magdalen, *Furnace of the Heart* (London: Darton, Longman & Todd Ltd., 1998), 92.

7. Dallas Willard, *The Spirit of the Disciplines* (London: Hodder & Stoughton, 1996).

8. Jean Vanier, *From Brokenness to Community* (Mahwah, N.J.: Paulist Press, 1992), 45.

CHAPTER 7   MAKING THE PILGRIMAGE PART OF DAILY LIFE

1. Alan Jones, *Passion for Pilgrimage* (San Francisco: Harper & Row, 1989), 37.

2. Kenneth Leech, *The Eye of the Storm* (London: Darton, Longman & Todd Ltd., 1992), 195.

3. I found this story in Sue Monk Kidd's *When the Heart Waits* (San Francisco: HarperCollins, 1990).

4. Morton Kelsey, *Caring* (Mahwah, N.J.: Paulist Press, 1981).

About the Author

TREVOR HUDSON is married to Debbie, and together they are the parents of Joni and Mark. He has been in the Methodist ministry for over thirty years, spending most of this time in and around Johannesburg. Presently, he is part of the pastoral team at Northfield Methodist Church in Benoni, where he preaches and teaches on a weekly basis. He is deeply committed to the work and ministry of the local congregation and believes strongly that for something to be real it must always be local.

Trevor travels internationally and leads conferences, retreats, and workshops in a number of diverse settings. He has written seven books, including *Journey of the Spirit,* which was awarded Best Christian Book of the Year of 2003 in South Africa. Among the others, *Signposts to Spirituality* is now in its ninth edition, while *The Serenity Prayer* has been translated into a number of other languages. His most recent book, *One Day at a Time,* will be released in May of this year.

Trevor's interests include watching sports, walking, discovering new places, reading, and a host of other activities he doesn't have time to do! One of his life's main enjoyments involves hanging out with his family at the local Italian restaurant, enjoying Arrabiata fettucine followed by ice cream and chocolate sauce.